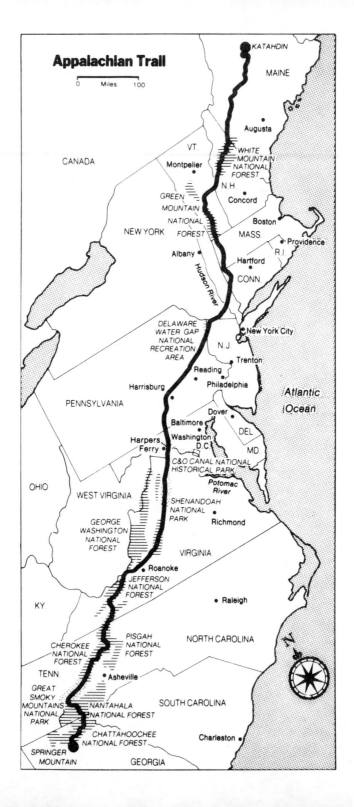

The Appalachian Trail Backpacker

Also by Victoria and Frank Logue

Appalachian Trail Fun Book
The Best of the Appalachian Trail: Dayhikes
The Best of the Appalachian Trail: Overnight Hikes

Also by Victoria Logue

Backpacking in the '90s: Tips, Techniques and Secrets

The
Appalachian Trail
Backpacker

(revised edition of *The Appalachian Trail Backpacker's Planning Guide*)

by *Victoria and Frank Logue*

Menasha Ridge Press
Birmingham, Alabama

All rights reserved
Printed in the United States of America
Published by Menasha Ridge Press
Second Edition, Seventh Printing, 2000

Library of Congress Cataloging-in-Publication Data
Logue, Victoria, 1961-
   The Appalachian Trail backpacker/by Victoria and Frank Logue—
Rev. ed. of: The Appalachian Trail backpacker planning guide
      p. cm.
   Includes bibliographical references (p. 181).
   ISBN 0-89732-161-8
   1. Backpacking—Appalachian Trail—Guide-books. 2. Appalachian
Trail—Description and travel—Guide-books. I.–Logue, Frank, 1963-
II. Title.
GV199.42.A68L64—1990
917.4—dc20
                                                    90-38907
                                                    CIP

Menasha Ridge Press
700 South 28th Street, Suite 206
Birmingham, Alabama 35233
(800) 247-9437
www.menasharidge.com

To our parents, John and Laura Campbell, Tom and Judy Logue, and Bob and Deborah Steele. Without their help and encouragement our thru-hike and this book would not have been possible.

◆ Contents ◆

◆ Acknowledgments ◆

The first edition of this book was written with the help of 26 thru-hikers, all of whom had recent knowledge of the trail. Our combined experience totaled more than 70,000 miles of hiking on the Appalachian Trail, with 50,000 of those miles occurring in 1988 and 1989. The hikers who supplied the information ranged in age from 18 to 57 and hailed from 13 different states.

Special thanks go to Bill and Laurie Foot, who gave much of their time and energy to the production of this book, and to Mark Carroll, Steve Marsh and Aaron Smith for their illustrations.

The following thru-hikers allowed us to draw from their varied experiences in compiling the information for the first edition of this book: Alan Adams, Edwin Carlson, Craig and Sondra Davis, Douglas Davis, Mark Dimiceli, Bob Dowling, Bob Fay, Bill and Laurie Foot, Todd Gladfelter, Phill Hall, Richard and Nancy Hill, Peter Keenan, Craig Jolly, Kurt Nielsen, Syd Nisbet, Allen Sanders, Peter Scal, Aaron Smith, Donald Waddington, Rob White and Mac Wrightington.

For the second edition of the book, we relied on the recent Appalachian Trail experience of Mary and Cal Batchelder, Bruce Campbell, Joe and Monica Cook, David Denton, Bill O'Brien, Nancy and Ted Peach, and Andrew Sam. All of these hikers have hiked extensively since our book was first published. Most have thru-hiked the A.T. at least once in the 1990s. They added another 25,000 miles of experience for us to draw from in creating the book.

◆ 1 ◆
Following the Blazes

"That's the Appalachian Trail," a tow-headed little boy of about 12 informed his younger sister. He was pointing across the road to a bronze plaque bearing the image of a hiker and the words, "Appalachian Trail—Georgia to Maine—A footpath for those who seek fellowship with the wilderness."

"People start hiking right there and go that way (he was pointing south) all the way to Maine," he told his wide-eyed sibling.

"What's Maine?"

Her brother, spreading his hands in the air as if diagraming a map of the United States, explained patiently, "You know when you look at a map of the United States? Florida's the part that sticks out down here and Maine is the part that sticks out up top. You know, people walk into the woods here and come out in Maine."

They were standing in the parking lot of the Walasi-yi Center at Neel's Gap in Georgia. It was a beautiful March

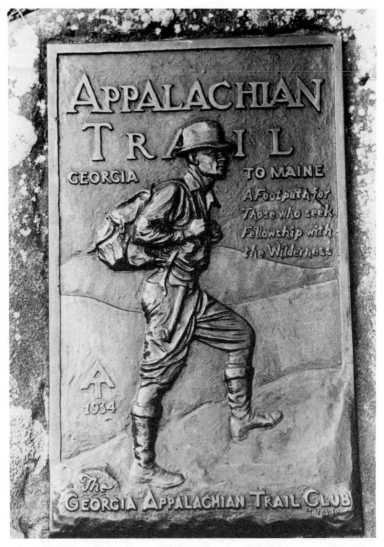

This plaque marks the southern terminus of the Appalachian Trail on Springer Mountain in northern Georgia. Springer lies at the southern end of the Blue Ridge.

photo by Frank Logue

day—the kind of winter's day you only see in the South. My husband, Frank, and I were about to begin our fifth day of hiking north from Springer Mountain toward Mt. Katahdin.

The youth was slightly misinformed. At Neel's Gap we were already 30.7 miles into the Appalachian Trail. But he had the vision, the sense of adventure that has appealed to hikers for more than 50 years: entering the woods in Georgia and coming out on top of Mt. Katahdin in Maine more than 2,100 miles later.

That vision is not limited to those who wish to go the distance. Within a day's drive of half the nation's population, the Appalachian Trail provides solitude and the chance to commune with nature for several million people every year.

Creation of the Appalachian Trail

The trail, which winds through the Appalachian Mountains of 14 Eastern states, was the vision of Benton MacKaye (Kaye rhymes with sky) and others who had kicked around the idea for more than ten years. In 1921, MacKaye took the initiative and launched the project through an article in *The Journal of The American Institute of Architects.*

MacKaye's original intent was to construct a trail from "the highest peak in the North to the highest peak in the South   from Mount Washington (New Hampshire) to Mt. Mitchell (North Carolina)."

He had a fourfold plan—the trail, shelters, community camps, and food and farm camps. The camps never came about. Although MacKaye's larger economic plan for the Appalachian Trail never gained support, its main purpose—an opportunity for American families to commune with nature—is the reason for the trail's existence today.

"There would be a chance to catch a breath, to study the dynamic forces of nature and the possibilities of shifting to them the burdens now carried on the backs of men . . . Industry would come to be seen in its true perspective—as a means in life and not as an end in itself."

MacKaye's words were echoed more than 60 years later by Appalachian Trail thru-hikers Bill and Laurie Foot, who wrote at the completion of their trek:

"We both discovered that we are in no hurry to get off the trail and rejoin the rat race . . . We found ourselves talking about how the trail had changed us . . . We felt that our priorities had changed and so had our outlook on life. We felt more confident of our abilities, more wanting to help others. We wanted to take the time to reach out to others."

Less than a year after MacKaye's article appeared in the architectural journal, the New York-New Jersey Trail Conference began work on a new trail with the goal of making if part of the Appalachian Trail. In the Hudson River Valley, the new Bear Mountain Bridge would connect the future New England trail with Harriman State Park and, eventually, Delaware Water Gap in Pennsylvania.

In 1925 MacKaye and others formed the Appalachian Trail Conference to guide the project to completion. By 1936, Myron H. Avery, president of the Appalachian Trail Conference for 20 years, had finished measuring the flagged route of the Appalachian Trail, and became the first 2,000-miler a year before the completion of the trail.

On August 14, 1937, CCC workers cleared the final link in the 2,025-mile-long Appalachian Trail. On a high ridge connecting Spaulding and Sugarloaf mountains in Maine, a six-man CCC crew cut the last two miles of trail. The route of the Appalachian Trail was not as originally envisioned by MacKaye; it was longer, stretching from Mt. Oglethorpe (the southern terminus of the Appalachians) in Georgia to Mt. Katahdin in Maine's Baxter State Park.

The next year a hurricane demolished miles of trail in the Northeast, while the decision to extend Skyline Drive (under construction at the time) with yet another scenic route—the Blue Ridge Parkway—displaced 120 more miles of the recently completed route. It wouldn't be until the world settled down to rest from World War II (1951) that the trail would once again be made continuous.

The First End-to-end Hike

In April of 1948, Earl Shaffer packed his Mountain Troop rucksack and headed for Georgia. "The Long Cruise," as Shaffer referred to his trip, started on Mt. Oglethorpe and ended some 2,050 miles and four months later on top of Mt. Katahdin. The continuous or "thru" hike had been undertaken to "walk the war out of my system," as Shaffer, who had fought in the Pacific during the Second World War, would later write, and earned him the distinction of being the A.T.'s first thru-hiker. The dream, which would catch the imagination of the young boy at Neel's Gap nearly 50 years later, had been realized.

In 1948, many considered Shaffer's thru-hike a stunt, but the dream of long-distance hiking has become a fever since then and has spawned other long-distance trails, including the Pacific Crest Trail, which runs from Mexico to Canada.

Since 1948, when Shaffer's lone expedition carried him across construction- and hurricane-torn trail, the A.T. has seen many changes. Each year the trail undergoes relocations and other improvements to its route. This causes the trail's distance to change almost yearly. From the original 2,025 miles it has stretched to more than 2,100 miles; it was 2,142.9 miles in 1992, 2,155.1 miles in 1994, and 2,159.2 in 1996!

Legislation passed in 1968 and 1978 gave the National Park Service the power (and the money) to purchase and protect a corridor of land from Springer Mountain in Georgia to Katahdin's Baxter Peak. As of 1993, less than three percent of the trail remained unprotected.

A Brief Tour of the A.T.

The Appalachian Trail's southern terminus is on Springer Mountain in Georgia. The wooded summit is a mile from the nearest dirt road and is generally accessed by the approach trail from Amicalola Falls State Park, which lies 8.3 trail miles to the south.

The Georgia section of the trail is more than 75 rugged miles and includes many strenuous gap-to-mountain ascents and descents. The trail crosses few paved roads because it is isolated by Chattahoochee National Forest, one of the eight national forests the trail passes through.

At Bly Gap, the A.T. crosses the state line into North Carolina and ascends steeply into Nantahala National Forest with its mile-high peaks. From the Nantahalas, the hiker heads north over the Stecoah Mountains to Great Smoky Mountains National Park. The trail reaches it highest elevation in the Smokies. At 6,643 feet, Clingmans Dome is the north-bounder's first taste of boreal forest with its balsam firs and rarely seen mountain cranberries. North of the Smokies, the A.T. crosses several grassy balds, where the hiker is rewarded by impressive 360-degree views, and continues along the North Carolina-Tennessee border until it reaches Roan Mountain. Here, the trail leaves North Carolina behind on Grassy Ridge and enters Tennessee.

In Tennessee, the trail descends into Laurel Fork Gorge, with its breathtaking waterfall, and crosses the dam at Watauga Lake before traversing a long ridge (known to thru-hikers as the Tennessee Turnpike) into Virginia.

The A.T. follows the main street through Damascus, Virginia, a town renowned for its annual Appalachian Trail Days festival and its friendliness to hikers. Virginia is known

John Campbell on top of Blood Mountain, the highest point on the Appalachian Trail in Georgia.

photo by Frank Logue

for the ridges that the trail follows and for its length—more than a quarter of the A.T. passes through this state.

Virginia also boasts many impressive mountains. Mt. Rogers, in the south, is a beautiful combination of boreal forest and wild ponies in grassy meadows (the latter at Grayson Highlands). The Priest and Three Ridges in Virginia's Blue Ridge Mountains are the last 3,000-foot climbs until the hiker reaches Massachusetts. Finally, Shenandoah National Park is known for its gentle trails where the A.T. crosses Skyline Drive more than 40 times in 100 miles.

The A.T. leaves the longest state to enter the shortest: West Virginia. Here, with only 2.4 miles of trail, the A.T. crosses the Shenandoah River and passes through the historic town of Harpers Ferry, where the headquarters of the Appalachian Trail Conference is located.

Crossing the Potomac River into Maryland, the A.T. follows the crest of South Mountain Ridge, and 40 miles later enters Pennsylvania. Hikers reach the approximate halfway point of the trail in Pennsylvania, and although the true midpoint changes from year to year, hikers usually go ahead and celebrate here by consuming a half-gallon of ice cream at Pine Grove Furnace State Park. The A.T. meets the end of the Blue Ridge in Pennsylvania at White Rocks, its northern terminus. The trail then descends into the Cumberland Valley. Once noted for its 15-mile road walk, this section of the Trail has been re-routed onto protected land.

The third largest of the trail states, Pennsylvania, is also famous for its rocks. After crossing the Susquehanna River at Duncannon, the trail follows the eastern ridge of the Alleghenies to Delaware Water Gap. Trail maintenance clubs in this state joke about sharpening the rocks to torture hikers, and there are some areas (in particular, from Wind Gap to Fox Gap) that are reminiscent of walking on a bed of nails.

If you think of New Jersey as a parking lot for New York City, all your preconceptions will have disappeared by the time you reach Sunfish Pond, a small glacial lake only a few miles into the state. Surprisingly, the trail in New Jersey is more rugged and remote than it is in either New York or Connecticut. This more-than-70-mile stretch includes several tough climbs (Culvers Gap, Pochuck, and Waywayanda) and some beautiful trail through High Point State Park and rolling farmland.

From the Kittatiny Mountain range, the trail proceeds north through New York's 104 miles, crossing Harriman State Park and the Bear Mountain Bridge. Here the trail reaches its lowest elevation—176 feet above sea level. Continuing northward, the trail enters Connecticut on top of Schaghticoke Mountain.

The fewer than 50 miles of Connecticut trail are spent rambling along the Housatonic River and the Taconic Mountains. In Sage's Ravine, the trail leaves Connecticut for Massachusetts. After climbing Mt. Everett, the A.T. departs the Taconics for the Berkshires. Noted for its beautiful trailside ponds, the A.T. in Massachusetts also features the ascent of Mt. Greylock.

The Appalachian Trail and the Long Trail join at the Vermont border to follow the crest of the Green Mountains and its famous skiing areas for more than 90 miles. After descending Killington Peak at Sherburne Pass, the A.T. and the Long Trail part ways. The A.T. continues along rugged woods and farmlands until it crosses the Connecticut River at Hanover, New Hampshire.

After leaving Hanover, home of Dartmouth College and the Dartmouth Outing Club (DOC), the trail remains under the influence of the DOC for the next 50 miles as it tops Smarts Mountain, Mt. Cube, and Mt. Mist. With the ascent of Mt. Moosilauke, the hiker is introduced to the first above-tree-line climb and the breathtaking White Mountains. Here in the Presidential Range, the highest peak in the Northeast—Mt. Washington—is conquered. At 6,288 feet, Mt. Washington boasts the "worst weather in the world."

From the Mahoosuc Range in the south to the granite

monolith of Mt. Katahdin in the north, the trail in Maine covers more than 278 miles of lake lands, bogs, and alpine-like mountains. The state is best known for Mahoosuc Notch (0.9 miles of scrambling over huge boulders); the Saddlebacks and Bigelows with their rare alpine flora zones; the Kennebec River; and the One Hundred Mile Wilderness, which ends in Baxter State Park. The ascent of Mt. Katahdin is an impressive hike, whether you've just walked more than 2,100 miles or the 5.2 miles from Katahdin Stream Campground.

◆ 2 ◆

Food and Cooking

It was one of those days when the sun beats mercilessly against the top of your head. It was also one of those days hikers dream of: there was a soda machine right on the trail.

The Appalachian Trail at this point was US 206 near Branchville, New Jersey. We were in need of food as well, but it was still too early in the season for Worthington's Bakery to be open more than one day a week.

As we stood outside, sipping our sodas and pondering our next move, a car pulled up to the store.

"It's closed," the three of us said, unanimously, as the woman uselessly tried the door. She turned to us, and her eyes lit up as she spied the backpacks. We all groaned, inwardly. "The Questions" were about to begin.

And even though we were standing in front of a bakery in rural New Jersey, the first question, after confirming we were indeed thru-hikers, was "How do you get your food?"

"We eat live chipmunks," our hiking partner, Craig Jolly said.

This illustration by Aaron Smith, whose trail name is Meister Ratte (or Master Rat), shows what would happen if you really tried to eat live chipmunks.

Before I could laugh, the woman said, "Oh really?" and asked, "and how many miles do you average each day?"

I was dumbfounded. We could have told her anything and she would have believed us, but we talked to her for another 15 minutes, setting her straight with the truth before we walked on.

There are standard questions a thru-hiker is always asked, and the main concern is, without fail, food. So, while on the one hand people worry whether you're getting enough to eat, on the other hand they half expect you to be subsisting off nuts, berries, and even (gag!) live chipmunks.

"We bite their heads off and suck their guts out," my husband joked later.

I'll have to admit that purchasing food was our main concern before hiking the Appalachian Trail. How much would we have to carry? Would we be able to find it often enough? Should we send some ahead just in case?

Fortunately, food turned out to be much less of a problem than things like weather, water, and insects.

Since live chipmunks are hardly appetizing (besides, have you ever tried to catch one?), what will you eat? Most hikers avoid specially packaged, dehydrated foods because the small portions for the prohibitive cost do not fit into most hikers' budgets. Here's what hikers really eat:

Suggested Breakfasts
Cold cereal with powdered milk
Oatmeal (The Fruit and Cream variety by Quaker was a favorite)
Toaster pastries (such as Pop Tarts)
Eggs (will keep for several days)
Bread with peanut butter
Bagels with cream cheese (cheese also keeps for several days)
Snickers candy bars
Granola bars
Gorp in powdered milk
Pancakes (bring the dry mix, add powdered milk and water)
Granola in powdered milk
Instant hash browns

Suggested Lunches
Sardines
Cheese
Nuts
Crackers
Beef jerky
Peanut butter and jelly sandwiches
Dried soups
Candy bars

Pepperoni
Graham or other type cracker and peanut butter
Sausage
Apples, oranges, and other fresh fruit
Lipton noodles and sauce
English muffins and peanut butter
Crackers and tuna
Corned beef or Spam
Dried fruit (including rolls, bars, etc.)
Cheese sandwiches
Granola bars
Snack foods (Little Debbie brand is especially popular)
Gorp (a mixture of dried fruit, nuts, M&Ms, sunflower
    seeds, etc.)

Suggested Suppers
Instant rice dishes
Macaroni and cheese (a real favorite; meat or dried soup
    often added)
Lipton brand noodle dinners
Instant mashed potatoes
Stove Top or other stuffings
Chef Boyardee spaghetti
Instant soup
Ramen noodles
Pasta salads
Instant potato dinners (au gratin, etc.)
Tuna and other canned meats can be used with any dinners
    (Pepperoni, dried beef, sardines, fish steaks, sausages,
    and hotdogs also show up occasionally)
Instant gravies and cheese sauces can be added to rice and
    potato dishes for flavor

Beverages
Water
Powdered fruit drinks, such as Kool-Aid (can be bought
    unsweetened and your prefered sweetener added)
Powdered iced tea (often mixed with fruit drinks)
Powdered fruit teas
Jello mix can be used as a tasty, hot drink, which also
    supplies extra calories
Instant coffee
Hot tea
Cocoa/Hot Chocolate

Desserts
Instant puddings
Instant cheescakes
Cookies
Instant mousse
Jello or other flavored gelatins
Powdered milk (mostly used to add to other foods)

Spices and Condiments
Not everyone uses spices, and no one carries all of these; but
those who bring spices tend to use a variety. For their weight,
spices and condiments can add a lot to a meal.

One other point is worth mentioning about spices. Many
hikers reuse the plastic 35mm film holders to carry small
amounts of spices. Kodak says this is a bad idea. There are
chemicals in the plastic that can leach into your food. The
containers are not food-grade material and washing them out
won't help the situation.
Garlic
Salt
Pepper
Italian seasoning
Seasoned butter
Tabasco

Red pepper
Curry powder
Chili powder
Oregano
Cumin
Onion powder
Parkay or other brand squeeze margarine (these margarines
    last approximately one week in hot weather and almost
    indefinitely in cold weather)

Nutrition

Nutrition on the trail is a "Catch-22." While it is easy enough
to carry sufficient food to account for calories burned during
a day- or weekend-hike, it is difficult and often impossible to
do so for extended trips.

Karen L. Lutz, in her 1982 Master's thesis for Pennsylvania State University, examined the dietary practices of Appalachian Trail thru-hikers to assess their dietary adequacy.
"The findings of this investigation have shown that hiking the
Appalachian Trail is a very effective weight reduction en-
deavor," she wrote. "Because of the nature of the activity,
adequate caloric intake is extremely difficult to maintain."

Lutz observed that because long-distance hikers usually
restock once a week, the problem of maintaining caloric
balance becomes circular. "If the hiker carries a larger food
supply for a given time period," Lutz said, "he/she carries a
heavier pack and the caloric cost of doing so is increased."

To counteract the deficiencies in vitamin intake, most
hikers in Lutz's study took multi-vitamins during their trip.
To add extra calories, hikers used liberal amounts of oil and
margarine with their meals.

Food sources high in calcium are particularly important
to long-distance hikers, Lutz said. Powdered milk and milk
products such as cheese are good sources of calcium as are
sardines packed in oil. "While dried fruits (e.g. dates, figs and
raisins) aren't extremely high in their calcium content," she

said, "a regular and steady consumption can add greatly to the total calcium and vitamin A intake."

In her study of six long-distance hikers, Lutz discovered that although all six subjects demonstrated a change in body composition and nutritional status, the most drastic change was the loss of total body weight. The men, she discovered, tended to lose both fat and lean body weight whereas the woman lost fat and gained lean body weight.

Hikers always took advantage of restaurant meals whenever possible, filling up on carbohydrate-rich foods, she said. These feasts were important to hikers because they were among the few times they could fill their stomachs.

Phil Hall came up with an equation to determine whether a food was worth its weight in calories and cost: # calories ÷ # ounces = calories per ounce; price ÷ # ounces = price per ounce, and, subsequently, calories.

For example, a box of macaroni and cheese costs approximately 40 cents a box. There are 300 calories in a box (or per meal). At 7.25 ounces per box, there are 41.4 calories per ounce, carried at just over five cents for 41.4 calories (300 ÷ 7.25 = 41.38 and .40 ÷ 7.25 = .055 or 5.5 cents).

A little complicated for day-to-day use, but for weight- and cost-conscious hikers, this equation may be something to consider before planning a food-buying trip.

Vegetarian Fare

There are a number of good options that vegetarian hikers may want to consider. Textured vegetable protein (TVP) and vacuum-packed tofu pack well and can be used in place of meat. Bulgar wheat, quinoa (pronounced keen-wa), rice and couscous go well with dehydrated vegetables and make for a great vegetarian meal that can be cooked on a backpacker's stove in 15 minutes or less.

For slightly more adventurous cooks, falafil or Nature Burgers can be fried in oil in a small Teflon pan over your stove.

Buying Food for Long-distance Hikes

Hikers can purchase food for day and weekend hikes at the local grocery store. Those hiking short distances also have more freedom in the different types of foods they can carry. But it also is not unusual for long-distance hikers to carry fresh meat for their first night back out on the trail after a shopping stop.

If you are hiking for more than a week, will you be able to buy food along the way? Would it be better to send something ahead to a post office? The majority of long-distance hikers suggest using both methods. Buying some food ahead of time and some as you hike allows you to be adaptable along the trail and leaves some leeway as to where, and when, you stop. It also allows for much less preparation before the hike, and is easier on the support crew at home.

Leaving yourself the option to purchase food along the way eliminates the need to time your arrival in town to coincide with the hours of a post office. (It's nice not to have to depend on the U.S. Postal Service for food.) It also allows you to satisfy any cravings you may have!

Sending food ahead
Sending all your food ahead is a viable alternative, if you intend to keep to a strict schedule, and do not mind planning what you are going to eat weeks or months in advance.

Said Bill and Laurie Foot, "We sent ourselves large boxes every eight to ten days. When we picked them up we would pack what we needed for four or five days then put the remainder into a smaller package, and send it to a post office five days ahead. This way, we knew our schedule better and avoided problems with arriving in a town when the post office was closed."

Were we to thru-hike the A.T. again, Frank and I agreed that post office drops in expensive or poorly stocked towns would be an immense help. We would also send ourselves "C.A.R.E." packages filled with goodies such as candy, nuts, and other high-calorie treats. They can be sent general delivery to a post office along the trail. Write "Hold for A.T. Hiker" on the package and they will be held longer.

Syd Nisbet suggested that to help save money, thru-hikers may want to send food to the following locations, which are difficult or expensive places to stock up with a week's supplies:

Fontana Dam, North Carolina
General Delivery
Fontana Dam, NC 28733

Delaware Water Gap
General Delivery
Delaware Water Gap, PA 18327

Monson, Maine
General Delivery
Monson, ME 04464

For more information on planning food drops, the Appalachian Trail Conference offers a rip-out-the-pages book, *Workbook for Planning Thru-Hikes*, that can help in your preparations. The book also offers other good advice for long distance hiking on the A.T.

How often do you resupply?
From our polling we found that most hikers were able to buy or pick up food every five days. The average spread between food buys or drops was one to seven days, although some hikers were able to hike as long as 15 days on one food drop.

An alternative method to buying or sending food is burying food canisters along the trail. The method is seldom used because it is time-consuming and risky. Hikers must bury their food along the trail before their trip, and it is possible that the food will be found in the meantime.

Relocations of the trail (more than half a dozen during some years) may cause some caches to be lost to you, not to mention the possibility of your markers disappearing.

Packing Your Food

No matter how you plan to get your food, proper packing is essential. Hikers joke that the yellow-and-blue-makes-green Gladlock-brand plastic bags are one of the great backpacking inventions of our time. This might be a little exaggerated, but not much. In the interest of space, weight, and waterproofing, you will want to repackage your food into plastic bags. Whether attracted to the aesthetic appeal of the yellow-and-blue-makes-green bags or you go for the old-fashioned type, plastic bags are a must.

Sort your boxes and other packages of food into meals. Open the boxes and pour the contents into plastic bags of appropriate sizes. On short trips you can cut down on weight and space by adding the powdered milk, salt, pepper, etc. into the bag at home and leaving the condiments behind.

If you need the cooking directions, cut out the recipe and put it in the bag with the meal.

Food should always be placed in your pack where it's easy to reach. As noted in Chapter 5, you're more likely to want to get at your food more quickly than any other equipment (except raingear and pack cover). There are many days while hiking that are too cold or too wet to stop. With food at the top of your packs, it is easy to grab what you need and continue to hike. Also, the more there is on top of your food, the better chance of its being crushed.

Stoves

Using a campstove while backpacking is almost mandatory now because there are so many areas where fires are prohibited. Where fires are permitted, the woods around shelters and campsites have been picked clean of downed wood by other hikers. Fortunately, stoves are now lightweight and efficient as well as inexpensive.

MSR Whisperlite

The Mountain Safety Research Whisperlite is the preferred stove of thru-hikers we have talked to, and it is agreed that frequent cleaning made life with the stove much easier. It is quickly assembled and ignites easily.

On one trip, while sitting at the Clarendon Shelter in Vermont with a totally useless cleaning tool, we finally agreed we would have to replace the jet. It didn't work. We tried several times, back and forth with each jet, soaking the jets in our Coleman fuel, hoping to disintegrate some of the clog. Still no luck. We wracked our brains for something, anything, that might be as slender as the tool's wire. I took my sewing kit out and looked doubtfully at the needles. They looked too thick. But we tried one and were ecstatic when it slid all the way through the hole. Not only did it work, but it cleaned the jet so well that we didn't have to clean the stove again.

We suggest carrying two cleaning tools. They can break easily, and we made the mistake of giving our spare to another hiker.

Some more Whisperlite hints include

- Be familiar with taking your stove apart before you hike.
- Carry a repair kit and two extra jets.
- If you are using unleaded fuel (which MSR highly discourages, but we have done with success when no Coleman fuel was available), change the jet every five days. After changing the jets (see MSR instructions for details), clean the dirty jet with the cleaning wire supplied with the stove, and drop it into your fuel container. The next time you need fuel, remove the now clean jet to be used again.
- For easy lighting: open the thumb valve a little while looking and listening for the fuel to fill the bottom cup. Then, turn the valve off immediately. Light the bottom

Frank Logue checks water boiling on an MSR Whisperlite stove.
Photo by Victoria Logue

cup and let it burn out completely. Finally, light the burner area while turning the valve back on.

• Use the heat deflector and the wind screen to reduce fuel consumption.

The MSR Whisperlite can be purchased for about $50; it weighs 12 ounces.

The Whisperlite Internationale 600 has a self-cleaning feature built in. The stove has a weighted needle that is jostled around in your pack to dislodge minute particles from the jet and eliminate the clogging problems while you hike. The stove runs on both kerosene and white gas, such as Coleman fuel. The Whisperlite International 600 costs about $60 and weighs 14 ounces.

Optimus Svea 123

The Svea is very similar in performance to the Whisperlite, and once you've heard the Svea's distinctive roar you will understand how the Whisperlite got its name.

"The Svea is wonderfully reliable and has a high heat output," commented Bill Foot. "Buying the optional special cap with pump makes lighting it very easy. We carried the repair kit and didn't need it, nor did we ever have a clogged jet."

Peter Keenan suggested carrying an extra key or chaining your key to the stove. If it gets lost, it will be tough to improvise, according to Peter, who was forced to improvise with a pair of needle-nosed pliers.

The Svea costs about $65 and weighs just over a pound.

Coleman Peak 1 Multi-fuel

The Peak 1 Multi-fuel stove runs on both kerosene and white gas, although you must install a vaporizer to use white gas. The Multi-Fuel is a pump stove, and it weighs a bit more than most other stoves. The high-output stove will boil water quicker than most and is good at simmering, but it can be finicky. It is either loved or hated by its users. Repairs in the field are difficult.

The Peak 1 Multi-fuel can be purchased for about $60, and it weighs 1 pound, 2 ounces.

The Coleman Peak 1 Feather 400 and 442

This redesigned version of the Peak 1 Multi-fuel offers the same power as the older model, and although its name implies that it weighs less, it actually weighs a few ounces more. The Feather 400 weighs 22 ounces, has a fuel capacity of 11.8 ounces and costs about $40.

It makes up for the added weight with speed, boiling a quart of water in just over four minutes. It is also easier to light than the older model and only requires a bit of priming in really cold temperatures. The Feather 400 can be unstable with larger pots and can roll quite a distance if tipped over on a slope. Unless packed carefully, the on/off switch can be bumped to "on" causing quite a mess. This can be avoided if the stove is packed into its stuff sack, which is a good place to put it because it won't fit in most cook sets.

Similar to the Feather 400 in design, the 442 was built specifically to burn unleaded fuel although it will burn Coleman fuel as well. It also boils water in about four minutes, weighs the same (22 ounces) and has the same fuel capacity (11.8 ounces); but at about $50, the Feather 442 is more expensive than the Feather 400.

Peak 1 Apex Component Stove System

This stove from Peak 1 weighs less than any stove ever made by the company—19.2 ounces including stove, pump and fuel bottle. With its patented fuel-feed system, the Apex uses a pump that mixes the fuel with air so that by the time the fuel reaches the stove it's fully atomized. Therefore, there is no need for a pre-heating priming cup. The stove boils water in about four minutes. It also simmers exceedingly well.

The fuel bottle, which is part of the system, holds 22 ounces of fuel, but the stove works best if the bottle is no more than three-quarters full (about 14.5 ounces). And with the Apex you do not need cleaning tools because the stove is self-cleaning. The Apex also comes with lightweight, built-in wind guards. The stove costs about $50.

The Apex II is designed to burn unleaded gas, as well as Coleman fuel, weighs 18 ounces and costs $65.

Butane/Propane Stoves

Two popular butane/propone stoves are the Camping Gaz Turbo 270 and the Peak 1 Max Series stoves. These blended fuel stoves don't need to be primed, and reach maximum heat output immediately. Unlike earlier butane stoves, blended fuel stoves will work in the cold and can handle high altitudes easily. But the stove's fuel cartridges must be sent ahead along the trail on long distance hikes because very few stores near the Appalachian Trail offer the particular cartridges used by these stoves. Also, the cartridges are more expensive than other forms of fuel.

The Gaz Turbo 270 costs about $35, weighs in at 10 ounces without the fuel cartridge and boils water in about five minutes. Fuel cartridges for each stove weigh about 10 ounces.

The Peak 1 X-Pert weighs 14 ounces without the fuel cartridge and costs about $60. It boils water in about 3.5 minutes. Fuel cannisters are available in 300 gram and 170 gram sizes. The aluminum canisters can be recycled.

Other Stoves

MSR XGK II

The MSR XGK II stove is advertised to burn nine types of fuel and can probably handle more. Like Mountain Safety Research's other stove, the Whisperlite, the XGK II can be easily repaired in the field. The 16-ounce XGK II is a high-output stove designed for use on mountaineering expeditions. The XGK II boils water in about four minutes. For general-purpose hiking it would probably be overkill. At nearly twice the price of the Whisperlite ($80), it proved not as popular in our survey, in spite of its abilities.

Zip Ztove

The Zip Ztove is inexpensive and lightweight, and use small twigs, bark, pinecones, and charcoal as fuel. It runs a fan off a small battery that superheats the fire. One of the drawbacks is that heating food can take more time. But the stove burns well when dry, dead wood is fed into it. It will also burn green or wet wood, but smokes heavily.

This stove operates better in cold weather and high altitudes than do gasoline and propane stoves. Disadvantages include the possibility of a dead battery at a bad time or a burned-out motor rendering the stove useless. It also requires constant feeding of fuel. Trouble with the Zip Ztove is rare. Of the people we know who used the stove, no problems have occurred in thousands of miles of hiking.

The Zip Ztove Sierra costs about $50 and weighs 15 ounces.

Outback Oven
Not a stove, but an oven attachment for your backpacking stove, the Outback Oven makes backcountry baking easy. It is available in three models from the simple oven which uses your cookpot to the Plus 10 Plus which includes a 10" Teflon pan and other accesories. The Plus 10 Plus costs about $45 and weighs 24 ounces.

Fuel
Most hikers we questioned found that no matter what the stove type, a 16- to 22-ounce container of Coleman fuel generally lasted 7 to 12 days. In winter, because fuel consumption is up slightly, you can count on no more than a week's worth of fuel from any 22 ounces. In the summer, one container may last as long as two weeks. All white gas stoves work best if the tank is not filled to the top. On the Whisperlite, leave a couple of inches of air at the top of the fuel bottle. With the Coleman Peak 1 stoves, only fill the tank three-quarters full for best results.

No hikers ever experienced any difficulty purchasing fuel for their gas stoves. When trouble occurred, unleaded fuel was an available substitute. A number of hikers used unleaded fuel exclusively (particularly users of the MSR Whisperlite) without any problems, though this is strongly discouraged by the manufacturer.

Hikers using the butane cartridge stoves said about one and a half of the full-size butane cartridges lasted them a full week. These same hikers said they mailed the cartridges ahead with no problem.

The Zip Ztove's biggest advantage is that you don't have to carry fuel for it. Phil Hall said he experienced no difficulties finding fuel for his Zip Ztove. Neither did he have any problems with lighting his stove in the rain.

On Going Stoveless

Other, not quite as popular options are to eat only cold foods or to build fires. We met only a few hikers that depended on cold meals their entire trip. It is not an impossible option, although most hikers depend on their morning cups of coffee, and hot liquid is vital in cold, wet weather. Hikers who opted to go stoveless subsisted for the most part on sandwiches–both cheese and peanut butter–along with toaster pastries, tuna and cereal.

We met no hikers who depended only on fires to cook their food. While a Zip Ztove might be easy to start in the rain, we often had trouble lighting campfires in wet weather. Cooking over campfires creates other problems, including stability: a number of hikers lost their meals to the flames when an unbalanced pot tipped over into the fire!

Campfires were wonderful for the warmth they produced, and their smoke was indispensable during mosquito season. Still, although fires are fine for cooking in an emergency, stoves (because buying fuel never seems to be a problem) are the best cooking option when hiking the Appalachian Trail.

Should you decide to cook by fire, remember to check local U.S. Forest Service, National Park Service, or state park regulations concerning fires before you go on a hike.

Cooking Pots and Utensils

The cooking pot may seem innocent enough, but it is one of the hiker's most important tools. It is a multiuse vessel, used for boiling water for drinks and meals, for gathering water, for eating out of (instead of a bowl), and even for holding your stove while hiking.

Although hikers use both the one-quart and the two-quart pot, the two-quart is probably the most efficient. We met many hikers who found that the one-quart pot tended to overflow during cooking. The food that boiled over the sides was much harder to clean. Improperly cleaned pots can lead to an uncomfortable hike: they increase your chance of food poisoning (and serve as an irresistable lure to hungry animal neighbors in the night).

Most couples we interviewed carried nesting pots. We use one to cook our dinner in and the other to mix drinks in (and to warm drinks during the cold times).

Hikers in our survey were evenly split on whether they carried a knife, fork, and spoon or a lesser combination. We carried spoons and the Swiss-made Opinel brand disposable pocket knives with no problems. Single hikers tended to carry a fork, spoon, and a pocket knife and used their cooking pot as a bowl. Couples carried bowls, and no one used plates.

A three-inch lock-blade pocket knife or a Swiss Army knife proved adequate for the entire hike, though hikers usually said they were little used.

Cleaning Up After Meals

Cleaning pots, dishes and utensils is an absolute necessity. Many hikers have found out the hard way that giving cleaning the short shrift can result in severe gastrointestinal problems not dissimilar to giardiasis.

There are several reasons to clean your pots as soon as you have finished eating, not the least among them being the growth of bacteria. Dirty pots also beg for the appearance of pests such as raccoons, skunks, mice and even bears (not to mention the hardships caused by dried-on macaroni and cheese, which is worse than Super Glue to clean up).

The best solution is to carry a little biodegradable soap and a pot scrubber. Bill and Laurie Foot offer these suggestions: "Use two pots for hot meals. You should never need to cook food in your large pot. Its use is for heating water and rinsing dishes, only. Add your hot water to the entree in the smaller pot, and after you've eaten, add more water and some soap to the smaller pot to use as a washpan. The remainder of the hot water in the large pot becomes your rinse water."

Cleaning should be done away from the campsite or shelter as well as far from the water source.

Use your sleeping bag as a cooler on hot days by inserting already cooled soft drinks or water into the middle or your bag. The liquid will stay cold for several hours.

Frank Logue pauses to look out over Watauga Lake in Tennessee. This view is from the Appalachian Trail at a rock outcrop behind Vandeventer Shelter.

Photo by Victoria Logue

◆ 3 ◆
Water

We were in what we called a "hiker's state of grace" the morning we reached Potaywadjo Spring Lean-to. It was only 10 a.m. and we had already hiked more than 11 miles. The eight-foot-diameter spring convinced us of the need for an early lunch. Ice-cold, clear, pure and sweet, we didn't even have to mix the water with Kool-Aid. We regretted leaving that bountiful water source as we headed on another arduous ten miles to Wadleigh Stream Lean-to. That night we boiled our macaroni in beaver water. What a difference! When hiking the Appalachian Trail you will scoop stagnant water from mosquito-infested pools, beg water from private residences, and tearlessly cry over dried-up springs. Your trembling hand will hold a shaky Sierra cup beneath a pipe gushing clear, cold spring water. Tipped to your lips, you will cry with near ecstacy as the water slides cooly down your parched throat. Hiking, especially long distance, will bring new meaning to the simple molecular structure—H_2O.

When you're backpacking, you have to rely on water from a variety of sources as this illustration by Mark Caroll shows. Treat your water to ensure it is safe for drinking.

But whether there's too much or too little water, hikers always manage to get by. It just depends on how much you want to put up with. The longer you're out, the better the likelihood that you will be uncomfortable at some point. How much water you'll need, even how much you carry, is always a matter of personal preference. And though it may be difficult at times, you will not die of thirst on the Appalachian Trail if you use common sense.

Where to Find Water
The purchase of the Appalachian Trail Conference's *Data Book* is essential. It will tell you where to get water in regions where water is scarce. With this help for dry areas, you can then rely on the regional trail guides (also published by the

A.T.C.) elsewhere. (See Chapter 11 and Appendix 2 for more about these books.)

It's true that you cannot always depend on the *Data Book* or guidebooks. Springs can run dry and are often intermittent. The same goes for small streams. But local trail clubs often post signs at shelters to let hikers know where the nearest water supply can be found.

On the A.T. you will get your water from everything from a pump to a spring to a beaver pond. One shelter even boasts a cistern. Water sources vary from stagnant pools dribbling from their source nearly half a mile away from the trail (and downhill to boot!) to clear, ice-cold springs gushing forth in front of a shelter.

The higher you are the harder it will be to find water, although there are notable exceptions such as Lakes of the Clouds, in the Whites of New Hampshire and Thoreau Spring, only a mile away from Katahdin's Baxter Peak. Conversely, the lower you are the more water there is, and the more likely it is that you'll have to treat that water. Once again, there are exceptions to the rule: the awe-inspiring Potaywadjo Spring in Maine's lake country is one. The eight-foot-round spring looks like a swimming pool compared to the paltry springs of the mid-Atlantic.

But on a hot day, even a beaver pond can look good and it takes a lot of restraint not to dip your Sierra cup into the inviting liquid. I remember times I wanted water so badly that the sound of my last remaining drops of water sloshing about my canteen almost drove me mad. But I saved that tiny bit of water just in case.

Don't succumb to the urge to drink risky water before you've purified it. It is easier to carry an extra pound or two of water than suffer the discomforts of giardia and other stomach ailments that dehydrate you and cause you to lose your strength. And diarrhea and cramps are harder to handle while hiking.

How Much Should You Carry

Like everything else, how much water you carry is up to you. We carried between two and three liters most of the time. That was usually adequate. I can think of only a couple of times we were forced to eat cold meals for supper or go drinkless. Granted, there were a few times we spent more than half an hour waiting to fill our canteens as water dripped from an improvised funnel, but that type of situation is rare.

One to two quarts or liters is pretty standard when it comes to the amount of water carried constantly by hikers. As a couple, we found we used approximately two liters of water at each meal: boiled water for oatmeal and hot chocolate or coffee at breakfast, powdered drink mix for lunch, and boiled water for the meal and drink at supper time. We used the most water at supper because it was our biggest meal and the hardest to clean up.

By the end of our trip, we had developed the practice of constantly carrying a full liter of a Kool Aid type drink and a spare liter (or two, depending on the heat) of water. By studying the area ahead of you in the books mentioned above, you should be able to determine how much water you'll need.

What to Carry It In

Most people, when they think of camping and backpacking, picture the canvas-covered metal or plastic containers slung about the neck of the hiker. Fortunately, that type of canteen is as outdated as heavy canvas tents and backpacks.

We started out with canteens—aluminum and small-mouthed—and soon regretted that decision. They were cumbersome, often hard to fill, and difficult to get at. We eventually ended up with a Nalgene bottle. Its wide mouth was easy to fill (and to mix drinks in); it was also easier to drink out of and hold. We carried a one-liter Nalgene bottle, but they are available in a variety of sizes, and at least two bottles should be carried. The screw-on tops are also recommended. (There are some that have a plug and screw-on top, but these seem prone to leaking.) This type of bottle is the most popular variety seen on the A.T. Some hikers even wear special holsters that hold their bottles in an easy-to-reach position: no more stopping to get a drink! Also good for this purpose are the new drink bottles used by athletes—the ones you squeeze to squirt the liquid into your mouth through a spout.

A little more flimsy, but still a viable alternative, especially in a desperate situation, are empty plastic soda bottles. The one-liter size is used the most. They tend to leak a bit around the cap, but are great when a heat wave hits and you need to carry extra water for a limited time. The same goes for plastic milk jugs with screw-on caps.

Something extra (but worth it) to carry is a collapsible water bag. They're wonderful at camp because they hold more than enough water for dinner, cleanup, and sometimes even a sponge bath. Water bags, however, are unwieldy to carry filled in your pack as your only water holder.

Most distributors of water bags also sell shower attachments that connect to the spout. We bought one, but I'll have to admit that we never used it. It always seemed to be either too cold or else it was hot enough to actually swim.

Giardia

"During the past 15 years giardiasis has been recognized as one of the most frequently occurring waterborne diseases in the United States," said Dr. Dennis D. Juranek of the Centers for Disease Control in Atlanta. According to Juranek, Giardia isn't just a contaminant of beaver ponds or of the burbling brooks that flow through cow pastures (and you'll get your water from both). Anywhere there are animals, including humans, there's a chance of Giardia.

The disease is characterized by diarrhea that usually lasts

one week or more," Juranek said, "and may be accompanied by one or more of the following: abdominal cramping, bloating, flatulence, fatigue, and weight loss."

While most Giardia infections persist only for one to two months, he said, some people undergo a more chronic phase. Others may show several of the symptoms yet have no diarrhea, or they may have only sporadic episodes of diarrhea every three or four days. Still others may not have any symptoms at all.

"The problem may not be whether you're infected with the parasite or not," Juranek said, "but how harmoniously you both can live together, or how to get rid of the parasite (either spontaneously or by treatment) when the harmony does not exist or is lost."

Juranek said that there are three drugs available in the United States to treat giardiasis: quinacrine or Atabrine, metronidazole or Flagyl, and furazolidone or Furoxone. All three are prescription drugs; they are listed in the order of their effectiveness. If you are worried about picking up Giardia, you may want to ask your doctor about a prescription, especially if you intend to be out hiking for a week or more. We know of only one hiker who carried a prescription with him, and, fortunately, he did not need it.

Two of the hikers interviewed during our research for this book picked up Giardia while hiking on the Appalachian Trail.

Treating Water

Suspect water should always be treated, and according to Juranek, portable devices with microstrainer filters are the "only" way to filter out Giardia. To be safest, Juranek says, the filters should have a pore size of one micron or less.

"Theoretically, a filter having an absolute pore size of less than six micrometers (microns) might be able to prevent Giardia cysts of eight to ten micrometers in diameter from passing. But for effective removal of bacterial and viral organisms as well as Giardia, the less than one micrometer pore size is advisable."

General Ecology offers several water filters. The most practical for backpackers is the First Need, which has a pore size of 0.4 microns and weighs in at 12 ounces. The charcoal-based filter purifies a liter of water in less than a minute and costs about $50. There is an attachment available from First Need that allows you to connect the filter to a Nalgene-type wide-mouth bottle. It costs about $10, and makes the First Need much easier to use.

The MSR Waterworks is a very popular filter which uses four elements to screen contaminants to 0.1 micron. The Waterworks screws on to an MSR Dromedary water bag or a Nalgene wide-mouth bottle. This feature makes the filter easy to use. It filters a liter of water in about a minute, weighs 1 pound 4 ounces and costs about $140.

A third filter option is the PUR Explorer and its smaller and lighter brother, the PUR Scout. They screen out impurities up to 1.0 micron and also use a tri-iodine resin to kill bacteria and viruses. They are among the few filters currently claiming to remove viruses. The Explorer filters a little more than a liter of water a minute, weighs 1 pound 4 ounces and costs about $130. The Scout filters a liter of water in about two minutes, weighs 12 ounces and costs about $60. An optional charcoal filter removes the tastes left by the iodine and can also filter out other contaminants. It costs $20 and fits on both of the PUR filters. Another optional attachment, this one costing about $10, allows you to connect the PUR water filters to a Nalgene wide mouth bottle while filtering.

Another filter that removes viruses as well as bacteria is Outbound's Trekker Travel Well. It was developed from the filters carried by the U.N. forces. It filters a liter a minute, weighs 6 ounces and costs about $65.

Whatever filter you choose to use, first, remove large

particles from debris-filled water by filtering it through a bandana. This will save wear-and-tear on an expensive replacement filter.

Though they have become popular in recent years, the drawbacks to filters are their bulkiness, weight and cost. There are two other, lighter, ways to get rid of Giardia, both with their own drawbacks.

Giardia can be killed by bringing your water to a boil. According to Dr. Dennis Addiss, also of the Centers for Disease Control in Atlanta, water need not be boiled to kill Giardia, only brought to boiling point. Giardia is actually killed at a lower temperature; bringing your water to a boil is just insurance that you have killed the parasite.

Obviously, the drawbacks to heating water include the time and fuel it takes to boil the water as well as the time it takes to let it cool down. But if you're boiling the water for a meal anyway, you can be assured the Giardia will be killed. You do not have to account for altitude when you're boiling water to kill Giardia.

Iodine and Halazone can also kill Giardia. One tablet in one liter of relatively clear, not too cold water for half an hour will effectively kill giardia, says Addiss. The major drawback to this method is the taste. Iodine leaves a not-too-pleasant taste in your water. And, once again, you've got to play the waiting game.

One way to combat the bad taste, according to Addiss, is to add an iodine tablet to a liter of water, and, once it is dissolved, heat that water to boiling. Then, divide it into two or three containers and top those containers off with unpurified water. The heated iodine water more effectively kills contaminants and doesn't taste as bad once it is diluted.

Another way to get rid of the iodine taste is to leave your water container uncovered for a while; this helps to dissipate the iodine.

Some hikers use two or three drops of chlorine (usually

Steve Marsh's interpretation of the dangers of pond water.

in the form of bleach) to treat their water. According to Addiss and Juranek, this is not a very good idea.

"There are too many variables that influence the efficacy of chlorine as a disinfectant," says Juranek. Among those variables are water pH, water temperature, organic content of the water, chlorine contact time and the concentration of chlorine.

"There's just no way to be sure that you've accounted for all the variables," says Addiss.

When to Treat Your Water

When it comes down to the truth, most hikers take chances and don't treat their water, especially when the source is a spring or at a high altitude.

Water treatment steps range from doing nothing at all to boiling water to high-priced purifiers," said Bob Dowling, a 1988 thru-hiker and victim of Giardia. "For the most part, I felt confident about the water sources I chose. Then I caught Giardia from an area I considered the most pristine—the wilderness stretch in Maine. This set me rethinking my practices on drinking water. A common question you hear is 'How is the water?' the response usually being 'Fine.' How do they know? Did they test for Giardia or other contaminants? Hell no! How can you be sure? The answer is you can't be sure. A hiker must treat all water as suspect. What to do? Use some common sense to decrease the chance of contaminated water."

Best to Worst Sources of Water	Confidence
Faucet or hose	high
Piped spring	high
Unprotected spring (Look for animal tracks around the spring.)	OK
Streams (Consider source of stream: Does it run by civilization or cow pasture, or does it stay in protected wilderness. Also, how cold is it, how near its source, and how fast is it running? May need to be treated.)	low

Ponds or Lakes   none
  (Assume the worst; treat water. Take
  the time to be safe even if you feel
  lazy or tired.)

All hikers we spoke with agreed with Dowling's analysis, and though many rarely treated their water, almost all agreed in retrospect that it's better to be safe than sorry. Or, as thru-hiker Nancy Hill put it, "Do as I say not as I do."

It all comes down to a judgement call: when the source is questionable, you're the one taking the risk. Many hikers agreed that they were less likely to treat their water when they were tired, depressed, etc.

Drinking three full cups of liquid at each meal will help reduce the need to drink between meals. If water is available between meals, do drink, but moderately. Remember: the old "don't drink when hiking" rule is nonsense.

◆ 4 ◆
Shelters and Tents

Our first day on the Appalachian Trail we limped into Hawk Mountain Shelter just as the sun was dipping below the horizon. Scorning the shelter, we set up our brand new Sierra Designs Clip Flashlight. About 5 A.M. we awoke to the patter of drizzle against the tent's fly. Not wanting to pack up a wet tent, we frantically pulled the tent stakes, threw the tent in the shelter, and crawled back in again. From that night on, we stayed in shelters unless they were already full or the bugs were insufferable. It didn't take us but one night to find out how useful the trail's system of shelters could be. And, although we spent only about half of our nights on the trail in a shelter, we always appreciated the ease of slipping into a shelter for the night as well as the protection it could provide.

Shelters
The chain of shelters and lean-tos along the length of the Appalachian Trail is a blessing to hikers. From Springer Mountain Shelter in Georgia to the lean-tos at Katahdin

A typical Appalachian Trail shelter during peak season use.
Illustration by Mark Carroll

Stream Campground in Maine, the shelter system is an important part of hiking the A.T.

A shelter is often a welcome sight at the end of a day's journey. In fact, it is not uncommon for hikers to be looking around every corner for the shelter that marks the day's end as they hike their last mile. A lean-to can be a dry place to rest or seek shelter for the night during a storm.

Originally intended to be a day's walk apart, the distance between shelters varies from under a mile to more than 30 miles. The shelters are made in a variety of styles and hold anywhere from 4 to 20 people.

Most shelters have established water sources nearby. The source is usually a spring or stream, but may also be a pond or other source. Having an established source of water makes shelters a good place to camp even if you don't intend to stay in the shelter itself, and many shelters have cleared tent sites nearby. But don't count on it. Although a rare occurrence, it is possible that you might have to push on another couple of miles (sometimes in the dark) to find a decent camping spot after coming upon a full shelter with no available camping sites. Some guidebooks state whether or not a shelter has spots cleared for camping.

While the water source is identified, the water's purity is never certified. Treatment is up to the hiker's discretion, as discussed in Chapter 3.

There is a good deal of variety in the design of the shelters. For example, in Great Smoky Mountains National Park, you will find three-sided stone shelters equipped with fireplaces and wire bunks for 12 hikers, and with a chain link fence front to keep the bears and humans apart—a preferable arrangement, which is secured only when the gate into the shelter is shut. In the Smoky Mountains, many shelters do not have privys, though this is changing.

In contrast, the lean-tos in Maine are Adirondack style, three-sided wood shelters. They are constructed with trees felled on the site. All the shelters in Maine have established fire-pits and latrines. Most of these shelters have been built to accommodate six hikers, although some are larger.

Shelters can also be wooden or stone cabins. Many shelters have latrines, though there are very few in the Southern Appalachians—Georgia, North Carolina and Tennessee.

The shelter system would seem to be a perfect solution to a hiker's shelter needs. It's not. The shelters are available on a first-come, first-served basis everywhere along the trail except in the Smokies, where shelter space must be reserved. During the spring and summer, two to three spaces in each shelter along the A.T. in the Smokies are "reserved" for thru-hikers. Because thru-hikers are not required to reserve a bunk in the Smokies, it is possible you will find your "reserved" spot already taken by other thru-hikers or backpackers. You may have to camp outside the shelter or hike on to another one. In the Smokies, a thru-hiker is anyone who is hiking the A.T. beginning 50 miles before the park and ending 50 miles on the other side of the park.

Although space in the Smokies must be reserved by calling the park, the shelters are still free of charge. There are some shelters along the Appalachian Trail that charge a small fee. In Shenandoah National Park, during peak season—Memorial Day to Labor Day weekends—most of the shelters have resident caretakers who charge a fee of $1. It is much easier to go ahead and pay the fee rather than risk being fined for illegal camping (usually about $25). Rules include having to camp 250 feet from the A.T. and a half mile from any road, building, or developed area and out of sight of it. Not an easy task in the Shenandoahs!

Northward on the trail, there is no longer a fee for camping in Massachusett's Sage's Ravine, which is maintained by the Appalachian Mountain Club (AMC). And a number of shelters and camping areas along the combined Long and Appalachian trails in Vermont charge a $4 fee.

Blood Mountain Shelter, in Georgia, is a four-sided stone cabin on the mountain's summit. It was built by the Civilian Conservation Corps in the 1930s.

Photo by Frank Logue

Pine Knob Shelter in Maryland is of typical shelter design and construction. Made with natural materials, it is designed to blend in with the woods.

Photo by Frank Logue

These shelters and campsites, interspersed with free shelters and sites, are maintained by Vermont's Green Mountain Club.

The AMC maintains the system of shelters and campsites in the White Mountains of New Hampshire and Maine. As in the Green Mountains, not all shelters and sites charge fees, but those that do, charge about $5 per person. The AMC is also responsible for the hut system in the Whites. Reservations are required, although some hikers can work for lodging by calling ahead. Lodging ranges from $40 for a bunk and breakfast to $50 for a bunk, breakfast and dinner (1997). At Lakes of the Clouds Hut at the foot of Mt. Washington, it is often possible to reserve a space in "The Dungeon" by calling ahead from another hut no more than 48 hours in advance.

Don't wait too long, though. The small room in the basement of the hut holds only six hikers and can fill up quickly. There is a charge of $6 for staying there.

And, last but not least, in Baxter State Park there is a charge for staying at both Daicey Pond and Katahdin Stream campgrounds—about $6 at both Daicey and Katahdin Stream. Reservations are needed at both areas.

More comprehensive and up-to-date information is available in *The Appalachian Trail Companion*, which is edited by the Appalachian Long Distance Hikers Association and published annually by the Appalachian Trail Conference.

Shelters can fill up any day of the year (surprisingly, we saw our largest crowds in Maine's One Hundred Mile Wilderness), and although space is often available, one should never depend on it, especially in the southern states between late March and late April when the mass of that year's thru-hikers begin their trek.

Thus, hikers need to carry their own shelter. A tent or tarp is necessary (weather can change in an instant in the mountains) for spending a night out on the trail.

Finally, there are the shelter registers. Zen-ish observations, diatribes on trail maintenance, exaltations of the natural world, and autobiographical ramblings are among the scribbles and scrawls found in trail registers. The writings left behind by hikers range from the monotonous to the brilliant, but they all give some idea of the types of people who spend time on the trail.

Take, for example, this entry found in Bobblet's Gap Shelter in Virginia: "Onward I travel, looking for the perfect trail." The writer, Steve Marsh, continues, "You know, the one in the guidebook that says, 'In 30 feet begin slight descent for next 1,400 miles.'"

Started as a safety measure to pinpoint the whereabouts of hikers, trail registers (usually spiral-bound notebooks) have become an important link in a vast communications network. Trail registers offer hikers the chance to make comments to those behind them, and to get to know, sometimes intimately, those ahead.

Along the same vein, "trail names" can become an important identifier even if you hike on the trail only a few days a year. Trail names are the nicknames used by hikers to identify themselves in registers. During our six-month trek, we hiked with several Craigs, but only one Estimated Prophet—Craig Jolly. For some reason, trail names are much easier to remember than given names. They are more interesting and often give you some idea of the person who bears the name. For example, when Ed Carlson began the trail, he was under a lot of stress and very high strung. He decided to take the name of Easy Ed, hoping that he would change to suit the name. In his case, it worked.

The Appalachian Trail Conference has a couple of requests regarding these unofficial trail registers. Profanity should not be used because families hike the trail and read the registers; don't write anything you wouldn't want a second-grader to read. Also, refrain from berating trail maintainers' performance and the hiking styles of others. The trail maintainers do their monumental task on a volunteer basis and without their important work the trail wouldn't even exist. As for hiking styles, any hiking style is correct if it suits the person using it. If someone hikes much faster than you, it doesn't mean that person is going too fast; it only means that he or she is doing more miles in a day than you care to do. The same goes for those who hike fewer miles in a day. It's not a contest and there are no prizes, so the ATC asks that you keep your criticism of others to yourself.

With that said, remember how important other's entries can be to you. If you have something on your mind, don't be afraid to share it. After a tough day of slogging through the rain, a read through the register can be entertaining. On the other hand, entries that ramble on for more than a page often go unread.

To fulfill the registers' initial purpose of keeping tabs on hikers should an emergency occur, always give the date, the time of day, your name or trail name, and where you are headed next. This practice allowed me to be notified in New Hampshire within a few hours of my grandfather's death in Georgia, for which my family was grateful.

Tents

Almost any hiker you speak to can tell you of a time they were glad they had their tent. They could also tell you of a time they cursed it.

Carrying a tent allows a hiker more freedom of choice. If you are carrying your own shelter, you don't have to push on to the next lean-to or stop early when you feel like walking. And you won't be caught by surprise arriving at an already full shelter with a storm brewing overhead.

Kurt Nielsen said he always preferred a tent "even set up inside a shelter for bugs. I slept better and more comfortably, and didn't get bothered by other's habits—snoring, writing by candlelight, or talking late. Shelters were often grubby and crowded but they were better than a tent in storms."

Setting up a tent in a shelter is feasible only if there is enough room. There is a trail saying that goes, "when it's wet, there is always room for one more in a shelter." Don't be a shelter hog.

So with the need for personal shelter established, what type of tent do you need?

Strictly speaking, a large piece of plastic and some rope is all that it takes. During a recent Gathering of long-distance hikers in Pipestem, West Virginia, the subject of tents came up in a workshop for those planning to hike the A.T. Of the more than 40 hikers on the panel, all had hiked extensively on the trail and each one agreed that a tarp or tent is a necessity even when spending only a night or two on the Appalachian Trail. When asked what type of tent they preferred, the answers ranged from tarps to roomy dome tents (costing from $10 up for a tarp or tent, to tents costing more than $250). In each case, the hiker said that their tarp or tent had proven adequate.

Important Features of Tents and Tarps

When you set out to buy a tent, have some idea of how much time you will spend in it. The more time you spend in your tent, the more you will appreciate added room. Will you keep your equipment in the tent with you or store it outside? That's an important question. If you don't plan to bring your gear inside, you will need to at least plan how you will keep it dry. This had not occurred to us and forced us to change our hiking plans many times.

Weight

To balance out all the things on your tent wish list, remember that you will have to carry the tent. Weight is an important feature. Most hikers, when questioned, said that the weight of a tent was its most important aspect, leading a few to purchase a tarp and sleep screen. Carrying more tent than the trip calls for can be almost as much of a mistake as not having an adequate tent.

As a rule of thumb, try not to carry more than 4 pounds of tent per person. If two people are splitting the load, you will be able to carry a roomier tent more easily. Having one person carry the poles and fly, while the other carries the rest, is one way to split it up. Another would be for one person to carry all the tent and the other person carry the cooking gear and more food to compensate.

Weight is the major advantage to carrying a tarp. For example, the Moss Parawing weighs a scant 1 pound, 4 ounces with stakes. Doug Davis carried a two-and-a-half pound, 10-foot by 12-foot plastic tarp.

"The tarp proved to be lightweight, spacious, and waterproof, which was everything I could ask for," he noted.

Tarps and Sleep Screens
One of the problems with a tarp is that it doesn't keep the bugs out. When the mosquitoes or black flies start to swarm, you won't want to be in a shelter or a tarp. Some hikers who relied on tarps for shelter from the rain also packed sleep screens to keep the bugs at bay. The hiker can also use the sleep screen in a shelter, making it a versatile alternative.

Escaping from bugs is no joke, and most hikers agreed that a tent or sleep screen is indispensable when the mosquitoes, deer- and blackflies arrive to torture innocent hikers.

Room
The second most important thing to look for in a tent is roominess. Are you tall? Is there enough room to stretch out to your full length? What about headroom? Do you have enough room to sit up comfortably if you so desire? Decide how much room is important to you before purchasing a tent. Also, will you be cooking inside your tent? On cold mornings, it isn't unusual to see steam rising from beneath the flys of tents as hikers heat water for coffee and oatmeal. If you think this is a possibility (something we never planned on but ended up doing countless times), make sure the fly has enough space beneath it so that it won't ignite. Whenever possible, we placed a flat rock beneath our stove for further insurance.

Ventilation
Ventilation is another important feature in a tent. On hot, buggy nights there is nothing worse than being stifled in an airless tent. Many tents these days offer plenty of no-see-um netting for cross ventilation and protection from bugs. Should you be planning on cold-weather camping, this feature won't be necessary. On the other hand, if you intend to hike in most seasons, a good fly will compensate in cold weather for the extra ventilation needed in hot weather.

Waterproofing and Ease of Set-up

Hikers we spoke with agreed that waterproofing and ease of set-up are important features to consider. There is nothing more miserable than sleeping in a wet tent. The better the tent, the more likely you are to sleep dry. But there are some days that it rains so hard that no matter how good your tent, you're going to get wet. If that should be the case, just develop the attitude of Ed Carlson.

The shelter was full at Piazza Rock Lean-to, just outside of Rangeley, Maine. Fortunately, there were a few good camping spots, and Ed set up his Sierra Designs Clip Flashlight a couple of hundred feet from the shelter. It poured all night long, lightning flashing, thunder booming angrily in response.

The next morning, Ed appeared, smiling as always.

"Did you sleep well?" he was asked.

"Great," he replied.

"You didn't get wet?" we wondered in amazement.

"Oh sure, I got wet," Ed said, "but I slept like a baby."

That attitude is hard to develop, especially when it's been wet for several days. With no sun to dry your tent out, and no shelter space, you can end up sleeping in a soggy tent. But, on the Appalachian Trail, the likelihood of there being no shelter space at the same time that it is raining is pretty low. Several new shelters have been built in recent years to close in some gaps in the chain. The only section of the trail without a shelter for about 30 miles is from Waywayanda Shelter in New Jersey to Fingerboard Shelter in Harriman State Park in New York, 28.4 miles.

You will also want to consider how easily a tent can be set up and taken down—important when it comes to pitching a tent in the rain or wind. A free-standing tent is a plus over a tent needing stakes. It can be set up anywhere at anytime.

Other Factors
Several hikers noted the importance of the fly's design and durability as well as the durability of the tent itself. Should you plan to get a lot of use out of your tent, its strength and expected lifetime will be an important consideration.

Privacy is also important. A number of hikers say that they carry a tent for privacy and as a safeguard against weather.

Tents to Consider
For most hikers, a tent will be the most practical alternative for staying dry on a rainy night. Tents keep out the rain and bugs; they are warm on cold nights because your body temperature warms the tent (sometimes by as much as 10 degrees) and the tent itself dulls the force of the wind. Here are some of your best bets.

Sierra Designs Clip Flashlight
A list of suggested tents should start with the popular Sierra Designs Clip Flashlight ($170). A quarter of the hikers in our survey used the tent and they all loved it. It sets up well in the wind and weighs in at 3 pounds, 14 ounces. The Clip Flashlight requires four stakes, which, regrettably, can be a problem if you will be staying on a tent platform. For two people, the Clip Flashlight can be a tight fit. It is a tent for one person with gear, or two if you leave the gear outside. But, half of the couples we talked to used it with no problems.

North Face Starlight/Starfire
The Starlight is a light, two-person tent with excellent ventilation. It weighs 3 pounds, 4 ounces and is available in either a sleeved version or with The North Face's No-Hitch-Pitch System. The No-Hitch-Pitch version costs about $220 and the sleeve version costs about $235. An optional ground cloth made to fit under the Starlight costs $40.

The Stafire is the Starlight's big brother. It has the same basic design, but is 11 inches longer, 4 inches wider and weighs 5 pounds, 12 ounces. The sleeved version costs about $300 and the No-Hitch-Pitch version costs about $320.

A-Frame/Eureka

A good A-frame tent for most uses is the Eureka Timberlite. The 4 pound, 1 ounce two-man model costs about $185. The Timberlite also comes in a three-person size that weighs 6 pounds and costs about $220.

Dome Tents

If you're more interested in room than weight, look for a good dome tent; they are strong and roomy for their weight. You should look for one with a rain fly that extends beyond the door of the tent. Either a vestibule or protective hood over the entrance will keep the rain from coming in with you when you enter the tent. Dome tents come in a variety of designs for $100 to $500.

Typical of the range of dome tents available are the Eastern Mountain Sports Adirondack and the Kelty Quatro Mountaineer. The Adirondack sleeps two, weighs 6 pounds, 5 ounces and costs about $130. The Quattro Mountaineer sleeps two to three persons, weighs 7 pounds, 7 ounces and costs about $300.

Other Brands

The above suggestions are just a place to start looking. Quality tents can be bought from many outfitters. Brands such as Timberline, Stephenson, Walrus, Jansport, REI, and L.L. Bean are among the most commonly seen, although tents from discount stores such as K-Mart, Wal-Mart, and Sears have also been used by some hikers without complaint.

Sealing the Seams

Once you purchase a tent, you will need to seal the seams. Purchase a tube of seam sealer when you get the tent and follow the instructions on the tube carefully. Even the best tent will be useless in a storm if the seams haven't been properly sealed. If you intend to be on the trail for several months, sending seam sealer ahead will help you avoid a wet tent as the sealer wears with age.

Follow the tent manufacturers instructions on where and how to seam seal your tent. Always seal the seams in a well ventilated area.

Sealing the seams after you purchase a tent also gives you the opportunity to set up the tent before you take it into the woods for the first time–perhaps saving you the frustration of learning how to set up the tent in a rainstorm or with darkness coming.

Ground Cloths

We didn't think we'd need a ground cloth and found out our first night on the trail that we were wrong. A plastic ground cloth, cut to fit just under the bottom of your tent, may not completely protect the tent from the damp (or wet), but it helps. Ground cloths come in most handy when it comes to setting your tent up on ground that has been wet for days.

If the ground cloth is much larger than your tent, you are more likely to wake up in the middle of a rainy night sitting in the puddle that has formed beneath your tent. By cutting it to within an inch of your tent's width and length, you'll wake up much drier. Another possibility (rather than setting your tent on top of the ground cloth) is putting the ground cloth inside the tent, said Peter Keenan. The bottom of your tent gets wet, but the equipment and people inside stay drier.

Digging a trench around your tent can keep the rain from running under it but is hard on the environment; we recommend that you not follow this outdated practice. Also, we never met a hiker that had the time or the inclination for such a job. After a day of hiking, who wants to spend the time in the rain at the muddy job of digging a trench?

If you're searching for the warmest site to pitch your tent, try a spot 15 feet higher than a stream, lake or meadow. The slight change in elevation really can result in 15 more degrees. Also, the south and west sides of trees and rocks soak up sunshine during the day and radiate heat at night. Finally, cold air flows down a valley at night, close to the ground and into the mouths of sleeping bags! Face yours downstream, if possible; it will be a lot warmer.

◆ 5 ◆

Backpacks

On almost any day during the summer, you can find an array of backpacks lining the porch at the Appalachian Trail Conference's Harpers Ferry headquarters. In recent years, the packs on the porch are looking different. From the external frame packs in earth tones of past years, hikers have begun to switch to the bright, often neon tones of today's internal frame packs.

Choosing a pack is important, whether you're out for a day or for an extended trip. Although the hike is not for the benefit of your pack, you do have to live with it every moment that it's on your back. Advances in technology have made backpacking easier on hikers. Backpackers have come a long way since Earl Shaffer carried his frameless, heavy, canvas pack more than 2,000 miles.

External versus Internal Frame
As with other gear, your decision should be based on the type of hiking you plan to do, and more importantly, what makes

Victoria Logue uses both hands to balance herself while crossing a stile with a sometimes unwieldy external frame pack. Syd Nisbet is following close behind.

Photo by Frank Logue

you the most comfortable. Both packs have their pros and cons. The basic differences are these: the external frame is designed to distribute the weight more equally and has a high center of gravity; the internal frame pack is designed to custom-fit each wearer and has a low center of gravity.

The external frame pack is a good choice for established trails, whereas the internal frame, which first gained popularity among rock climbers, is better suited to rugged terrain or off-trail hiking.

Before buying any pack, you should test it first. The best method is to rent a pack and try it out on a weekend hike. Some stores even offer rent-to-buy programs. If you can't do that, see if you can't load up the pack you're interested in and try it out in the store. Many stores have sand bags on hand for this purpose.

Also, keep in mind that torso length is more important than overall height. For example, if a pack is suggested for someone six feet tall, it may actually be more appropriate for a shorter person with a longer torso—another reason to try on a pack before you buy it.

External Frame

Because you will probably carry as much for a weekend trip as you would for a longer trip, an external frame needs to have approximately 3,000 cubic inches carrying capacity. External frame packs come in top-loading, front-loading and combination models. A top-loading pack works like a duffle bag attached to a frame, whereas front-loading packs give you easy access to your gear. But most manufacturers design their external packs with both a top-loaded and front-loaded section as well as front and side pockets.

The most important feature is the pack's hip belt. The hip belt carries the bulk of the weight, so that a properly fitted pack allows you to drop one shoulder out of its strap without a significant change in weight distribution. This hip belt should be well-built and snug-fitting.

Many companies offer optional hip belts that are larger or smaller than the standard adjustable hip belt. Should you be planning a thru-hike, keep in mind that the hip belt that fits you when you begin may not fit you later in your trip. Keep the manufacturer's telephone number, often toll-free, in case you need to order another hip belt. Hip belts also are prone to breaking because of the amount of stress they receive. Should this happen, manufacturers are great about replacing them free-of-charge.

Manufacturers of external frame packs boast that the frame keeps the pack away from your body and thus is cooler in the summer. External frames also have mesh back bands, which should be tight and well-adjusted for your comfort.

Some manufacturers of external frame packs are Jansport, Kelty, Camp Trails, Peak 1 and The North Face. Of course, very good packs are sold under the REI, L.L. Bean and other distributor's brand names. A good external frame pack can be purchased in the range of $100 to $250.

Internal Frame

An average internal frame pack will need a volume of at least 4,000 cubic inches to be comparable to an external frame pack with a 3,000-cubic-inch capacity. This is because sleeping gear is attached to the frame of an external pack but is carried in a special compartment inside the internal frame pack.

Internal frame packs are equipped with harnesses, straps and other adjustments so that the pack may be form-fitted to each wearer.

Hikers who use the internal frame pack laud the upper body mobility that it offers. The ease of movement is most noticeable when hiking in areas like the White Mountains of New Hampshire and the Mahoosucs of Maine where rock-climbing, hopping and scrambling predominate the hiking.

The hip belt on the internal frame pack is form-fitted and is part of the pack; it is adjustable but is not optional.

Most internal frame packs do not come with external pockets. The majority are top-loading packs with a separate compartment for your sleeping bag.

Some internal frame pack manufacturers are Lowe, Gregory, The North Face, Mountainsmith, Dana Design, Osprey, Eastern Mountain Sports, REI and Camp Trails. These packs can be purchased for $125 to $425.

The Two-day Pack

Some hikers can live leanly enough to make long trips with the two-day type of pack. The advantages of the two-day pack are obvious–not only do you carry less weight but stress to your body is lessened. But the approximately 2,000-cubic-inch internal frame packs are definitely not for everyone.

"I know some people cannot live without certain luxuries," said Rob White, who was willing to give up the bulkiness of a sleeping bag by using a tablecloth instead.

Alan Adams also regularly hikes with a two-day pack, in which he carries about 20 pounds for each five-day trip. Adams said that by not carrying more than five percent of his body weight, he remains comfortable while hiking.

"Any more than that is work," he commented.

Adams kept his weight down by using a two-pound sleeping bag and sleeping under a fly rather than in a tent.

Once again, decide how much you can do without and still enjoy your hike before purchasing a smaller-than-average pack.

Pack Covers

Although all backpacks are made of water resistant material, moisture will seep through seams and zippers and saturate your gear if your pack is left unprotected. A pack cover can be anything from a heavy duty garbage bag, which will keep your pack dry when camping (and protect it from the dew at night), to a specially designed cover made for the purpose. These coated nylon or Gore-Tex covers, when their own seams are properly sealed, fit over your pack but still allow you to hike. They are usually fitted to your pack by elastic or a drawstring.

No matter what kind of pack cover you purchase, and you do need to buy one, you will still probably want to carry a heavy duty (BIG) garbage bag to keep your pack covered at night because pack covers are not designed to protect the straps and back of your pack. A plastic garbage bag is indispensable when you are forced to camp in a downpour but don't have room for your pack in the tent.

The poncho-style pack covers work under ideal conditions only. The poncho is designed to be a one-piece rain gear, covering both you and your pack at the same time. Not only do ponchos tend to tear up easily, but they work only when the wind is not blowing hard. Should the wind whip up, so will your poncho, and both you and your pack will soon be soaked.

How Much To Carry in Your Pack

An easy-to-use rule of thumb is to never carry more than one-third of your body weight. On shorter trips, it is wiser to carry even less–about one-quarter of your body weight is about right.

Some hikers swear that you should carry only one-fifth of your body weight, but that can be difficult to do, especially if you plan on winter hiking or are carrying a week's worth of food.

What if you pack your pack and it weighs 60 pounds and you weigh only 120? Unpack and look at everything very carefully. Items like your stove, tent and sleeping bag are

Two different hiking styles (and pack styles) meet in this illustration by Mark Carroll.

absolutely essential. But take a look at your clothes; you don't have to wear something different every day.

Another area people overpack in is toiletries. If you must shave, deodorize, shampoo, etc., try to find sample size containers. Don't bring a radio unless it's the compact "Walkman" type. Flashlights that are "hiker-friendly" can be purchased. A small flashlight that uses AA batteries will serve you just as well as one that uses C or D batteries.

Those are just a few examples. Chapters 8 and 9 also

provide suggestions on what to pack. Look objectively at what you've packed: Are you sure you can't live without it?

Packing Your Pack

Once you've bought a pack, where do you put what?

You're going to want certain items to be handy. Any system that you come up with will work as long as you know how to get at those necessary items quickly. If you are hiking with a partner, you may want items you need to get at quickly, such as a camera, in the side pocket of your partner's pack.

Rain gear, for example, will be something that you'll want to be able to lay your hands on immediately. It is not unusual to be caught in a sudden downpour, and if you have to drop your pack and dig through it to get at your raingear, you and all your gear may be soaked by the time you find it.

You will also need a means to carry water so that you can get at it without taking off your pack. Some hikers use holsters for their water bottles. This did not occur to us, but we kept our canteens within reach in a side pocket on our packs.

It also is important to distribute the weight as equally as possible. Don't put all your food on one side, for example, and all your clothes on the other. Believe it or not, food will be a good third of the weight you are carrying.

Packing the heavier stuff toward the top of your pack will keep the load centered over your hips, particularly in an external frame pack. On the other hand, don't follow this rule to its furthest possible conclusion because an overly top-heavy pack is also unwieldy. When packing an internal frame pack for hiking on rugged terrain, putting heavier items at the bottom will keep your center of gravity low and make it easier to maintain your balance when jumping from rock to rock.

Sleeping bags are usually secured at the bottom of an external frame pack, strapped to the frame just below the pack sack. In the internal frame packs, the sleeping bag compartment is usually the bottom third of the pack.

Another suggestion: you will probably want your food more readily available than your clothes and cooking gear, particularly at lunch time. Nothing is more aggravating than to have to dig through your clothes just so you can satisfy your craving for Gorp.

Fanny Packs

Another way of keeping things handy is using a fanny pack in conjunction with your backpack. Many hikers use these miniature packs in reverse, snug across their bellies with the strap fastened in the small of the back. Cameras, water, snacks, your data book, maps, guides, or whatever you need quick access to can be carried by this method.

Fanny packs are useful on day hikes for the same reasons. But they are not as comfortable as day packs, because they do not distribute the weight as well, and often cannot carry as much as you might like to bring on a day hike. Here, too, they can be used along with a day pack or alone, if you have a partner carrying a day pack.

Day Packs

Most day packs are made in the same teardrop style, so the important thing to look at is how well the pack is made. Inexpensive day packs can be purchased at any discount store, but if they are poorly padded and have little support, you won't have hiked a mile before you regret the purchase.

Leather-bottomed packs are the most durable and carry the load better by supporting the weight rather than collapsing beneath it.

Make sure the shoulder straps on your day pack are very secure because this is the first place that such packs fall apart. This occurs because you are carrying the weight on your shoulders as opposed to your hips. A number of day packs have extra reinforcement where the shoulder straps connect to the sack to prevent this from happening. Another feature to look for is padding at the back of the pack. The more reinforced the section of pack that lies against your back, the less likely it is that you'll be poked and prodded by the objects inside the pack.

By tilting your head sideways (so your eyes are perpendicular to the ground), you can improve your perception of an impending climb. Normally a slope will look easier or harder than it really is; this trick will put things in perspective.

◆ 6 ◆

Sleeping Bags

The barn, Yellow Mountain Gap Shelter on the Appalachian Trail, was swaying from side to side as winds in excess of 100 miles per hour whipped through the gap. It was cold and dark and there was a crusty substance on our sleeping bags we couldn't identify.

Frank turned on his lighter and we stared at our bags in disbelief. They were covered with snow, which had made its way through the cracks in the barn's walls. For the next 36 hours we were trapped in our sleeping bags, our only warmth and refuge from the storm that raged outside.

The storm that caught us in that Tennessee barn occurred on April 6. It is not unusual for hikers to see some snow in the South in April. Although it is doubtful that you'll be forced to remain in your sleeping bag for more than a day, a third of your life is spent sleeping so a third of your time hiking will be spent in a sleeping bag. That means it's pretty important to choose something you'll be comfortable in.

It's probably wise not to go for an extreme, unless you plan to buy several bags. Sleeping in a zero-degree bag (see Comfort Ratings below) on a muggy summer night in Pennsylvania can be almost as much torture as being in a 45-degree bag when you're snowed-in in the Smokies.

The trick is to find a balance point between comfort and practicality. There are several things to look for when purchasing a bag: comfort rating, filling and weight. Care and cleaning and the bag's construction should also be kept in mind.

Comfort Ratings

A comfort rating is assigned to most sleeping bags by the manufacturer or retailer. The rating, in simplest terms, is the lowest temperature at which the bag remains comfortable.

Unfortunately, most comfort ratings are overly optimistic. They assume you are an average hiker under normal conditions. The problem comes in trying to determine who is average, what conditions are normal, and what is comfortable. What it really means is that you are neither fat nor thin and you are not overly fatigued or sleeping out in the open. It is also assumed you are using a sleeping pad and that you have a normal metabolism.

Keeping all that in mind, comfort ratings are helpful when compared to each other. A 10-degree bag will keep you warmer than a 20-degree bag.

Before deciding on a comfort rating, try to determine the range of temperatures you will be hiking in. If you intend to do a lot of cold-weather camping, you'll probably want a bag rated between 0 and 20 degrees. What if your hiking will take you through both cold and hot weather? You may want to buy a 20-degree bag and a bag liner, which can raise your bag's temperature by as much as 15 degrees. (Bag liners are covered later in this chapter.) Of course, if money is no object, you may prefer to buy several bags with ratings ranging from 0 to 45 degrees or so.

A 20-degree bag is probably adequate for three-season camping, according to most of the hikers we polled. Several even said that their 20-degree bag was perfect for the entire Georgia to Maine trek, although most said it could get a bit chilly when the temperature dipped below freezing.

Fillings

When it comes to backpacking, there are seven fillings to consider when purchasing a bag. They are the lightest and warmest to be found on the market, currently: Quallofil, Hollofil II, Lite Loft, Micro-loft, Polarguard HV, Primaloft and down.

Quallofil

The fibers of this polyester filling are hollow, each with four microscopic tubes that allow for a greater insulating ability and more surface area. Quallofil, which is as soft as down, is nonallergenic, and retains most of its loft when wet. Loft is the thickness of the filling. In other words, when Quallofil gets wet it doesn't mat or become thin and hard, or lose its warmth.

Hollofil

Also polyester, Hollofil fibers are about two inches long and must be sewn to another backing to prevent clumping, which leads to cold spots in a sleeping bag. Similar to Quallofil, Hollofil has a single hole in the fiber; but it allows for more "air" per ounce and thus provides more insulation. The added insulation is gained at a price because the backing materials used for the filling mean added weight. Like other polyester fills, Hollofil loses only about a tenth of its warmth when wet.

Hollofil II has silicone added to make the fibers easier to compress and the bag, therefore, easier to fit into a stuff sack.

It's important to get a sleeping bag you feel comfortable with.
Illustration by Mark Carroll

Lite Loft

Thinsulate Lite Loft by 3M is the warmest synthetic insulation available for its weight. Consisting of microfine polyester/olefin fibers, Lite Loft is heat-bonded into a fluffy laticework. Its fibers are said to trap heat more efficiently than other synthetics. Also, this new filling is said to be lightweight, even when wet, and easily compressible.

Microloft

This is the latest from DuPont. Microloft boasts the smallest of the micro fibers—thinner than a human hair. These tiny polyester fibers enable the filling to trap more heat while remaining soft and supple.

Polarguard HV

This polyester filling's biggest advantage is that it is a continuous filament. This means that the fibers, which are long and interwoven, don't become matted. Without the need for a backing to prevent cold spots, Polarguard HV bags can be made for a lower comfort rating without the added weight. PolarGuard HV also retains its loft, and thus its warmth, when wet. Polarguard HV is 20 percent warmer than the old Polarguard for the same weight, due to hollow fibers which cut back the weight by 25 percent.

Primaloft

The U.S. Army developed this filling while doing research. With tiny fibers interspersed with stiffer fibers, Primaloft mimics the structure of goose down. Unlike down, Primaloft is water repellant and retains its warmth when wet better than most synthetic fillings.

Down

Down has long been lauded, and is still number one, when it comes to providing maximum warmth and comfort for minimum weight and bulk. Down sleeping bags breathe better than polyester fiber bags, and are less stifling in warmer temperatures than their synthetic counterparts. But when a down bag gets wet, it loses almost all of its warmth and gains much more in weight than synthetic bags. With proper care, down bags retain loft longer than synthetic-filled bags.

Warmth When Wet

According to tests conducted by Recreational Equipment Incorporated (REI), "a synthetic bag will lose about 10 percent of its warmth while gaining about 60 percent in weight" when the sleeping bag gets wet. Conversely, they said, a water-soaked, down-filled bag "will lose over 90 percent of its warmth, gain 128 percent in weight and take more than a day to dry."

What this all means is that your ability to keep a down bag dry is a major factor in purchasing a bag. Down bags are clearly a favorite with thru-hikers we've surveyed, followed closely by Hollofil, Quallofil, and Polarguard, respectively. All four fillings had strong proponents, though the newer fillings, such as Lite Loft are starting to gain ground quickly.

Weight

The lighter your bag the better. But, unfortunately, the lighter the bag the more it's going to cost. Try not to buy a bag that weighs more than 5 pounds. A bag in the 2 to 4 pound range is probably your best bet for cost-efficiency and warmth.

Weight is determined by the comfort rating and the filling: usually, the lower the comfort rating, the more the bag weighs. Fillings other than the seven mentioned here also weigh a lot more than you'll be willing to carry.

Keep in mind that it is likely that the bag you buy will eventually get wet, and that that will increase its weight somewhat.

Compatibility

For couples interested in hiking together, some sleeping bags may be zipped together. Many sleeping bag manufacturers offer bags with right and left zippers. Both mummy bags and barrel-shaped bags can be purchased with compatible zippers. Mummy bags are contoured to your body, and include a hood for your head. Barrel-shaped bags taper at the feet but don't have a hood and are, consequently, not as warm.

Bag Shell/Liner

Several manufacturers are working with DryLoft, a shell material made by W.L. Gore and designed to take the place of Gore-Tex in sleeping bags and parkas. Gore claims the material is twice as breathable without compromising water resistance.

Another material gaining popularity is DuPont's Coolmax, used to line some sleeping bags. Not to be confused with optional bag liners discussed below, this is the bag's permanent inner lining. Coolmax is designed to wick water out of the interior of the bag.

Bag Liners

Purchasing a bag liner is a good way to warm up your bag without adding much cost or weight. There are three types of bag liners—over bags, vapor barriers and plain inner liners.

The over bags slide on over your sleeping bag and have a filling that increases the warmth of your bag by as much as 20 degrees. They cost approximately $50 to $100 and weigh about 2 to 3 pounds–kind of bulky for extensive backpacking but not too bad for short, cold-weather trips.

Vapor barrier liners are inserted inside your sleeping bag and can raise its temperature by as much as 15 degrees. Basically, with the vapor barrier, you're sticking yourself inside a plastic bag. They are constructed out of coated nylon or other materials, and weigh only 5 to 6 ounces or so. They also cost much less than the over bags—approximately $20 to $30 a bag. The drawback to the vapor barrier is comfort; they are designed to make you sweat and thus use your own warmth to keep you warm. Vapor liners are recommended for temperatures well below freezing.

You can also purchase simple bag liners made of flannel, cotton, breathable nylon, synthetics, and down for anywhere from $5 to $100, and weighing from 3 ounces to 2 pounds. The degree to which they warm your bag varies and should be clarified by the salesperson before you decide to purchase such a liner.

Caring For and Storing Your Bag

Synthetic sleeping bags can be washed by hand or in a commercial washer, with warm or cold water. They should be washed with a mild soap such as Ivory, and, if not air dried, should be dried at a low setting in your dryer. Nikwax offers a line of products specifically made to clean down and synthetic bags, while retaining loft. They are available in many backpacking stores.

Down sleeping bags should be hand washed. If washed in a machine, your bag could lose its loft because the detergent breaks down the natural oils of the goose down. Down bags should not be dried in a household dryer; rather, they should be drip dried for several days. The bag can then be placed in a commercial dryer on low heat to fluff it up. Throwing in a clean pair of tennis shoes will break up matted down.

Sleeping bags should not be stored in the tiny stuff sacks that they are normally carried in on a hike. A big, loose bag is the best way to keep your bag in good condition when you're not on the trail. Stuffing your bag into a small sack every day while hiking is all right because you're taking your bag out almost every night. But if you store it that way at home, the filling becomes packed together and it is hard to restore its loft.

Sleeping Pads

Sleeping pads are a necessity. If you don't sleep on a pad, you lose all your heat to the ground. And, although the padding is minimal, they really are more comfortable than a shelter floor or the hard earth.

The two sleeping pads favored by hikers are the Therm-a-Rest and the Ridgerest. The Therm-a-Rest is a self-inflating pad that can be purchased in three-quarters or full length. It is the overwhelming favorite among hikers, although it weighs and costs more than the Ridgerest. The three-quarter pad weighs 1.5 pounds and costs about $45, and the full-length pad weighs 2.25 pounds and costs about $60. Therm-a-Rest pads are also available in deluxe models, which come with a repair kit and stuff sack. Most hikers find the three-quarter length pad sufficient for their comfort. The Therm-a-Rest is an open-cell foam pad with a nylon cover.

A "couples kit" can be purchased for the Therm-a-Rest that allows two pads to be joined together. It is simply two nylon tarps that hold the pads so that they do not move around in the night.

The Ridgerest, although less popular among hikers we know, was awarded *Backpacker Magazine's* product design award. It, too, can be purchased in three-quarter and full length. The three-quarter pad weighs 9 ounces and costs about $13. The full-length pad weighs 14 ounces and costs $16. The "ridges" in the Ridgerest were designed to trap air to keep you warmer. It is a closed-cell foam pad.

The Basic Designs Equalizer, like the Therm-a-Rest, is a self-inflating pad. It features interconnecting chambers that change shape as you move. The three-quarter length Equalizer weighs 35 ounces and costs about $50.

Other options are also available, including the blue foam pads available at most camping stores and other foam pads. These pads weigh anywhere from 8 ounces to 16 ounces and can be purchased in the $10 to $15 range.

Pack your sleeping bag into a garbage bag before loading it into its stuff sack. This will keep the day's rain from ruining a good night's sleep. This is critical with down sleeping bags, which loose their ability to insulate when wet. If you will be fording a stream or are expecting hard rains, put the stuff sack into another bag to doubly protect your sleeping bag.

◆ 7 ◆
Footgear

About ten miles out of Elk Park, North Carolina (the day after a snowstorm trapped us in a barn for 36 hours), Frank noticed that the soles were falling off his boots.

That night, at Moreland Gap Shelter, we worried about how we were going to make it to the next telephone. Fortunately, a fellow hiker, Craig Watkins, happened to have some duct tape. 18 miles later we found a handy telephone and had my mother send some boots, next-day mail, to Damascus, Virginia, 39 miles away.

We made it to Damascus in two days, walking the last 18 miles in snow. The new boots didn't; somehow they got lost on their way to Damascus. But four days later we were on our way again.

Almost every experienced hiker can tell you a boot story. We know of only three hikers who hiked the whole A.T. on one pair of boots, and two of those wore Limmers, boots that are custom-made for just over $200.

Frank Logue's New Balance Cascades were duct taped together after the soles started to separate in Tennessee. Other hikers have used the same boot without similar problems.

Photo by Frank Logue

Boot Weight

Your choice of boots will depend on where and when you want to hike, and how often. Lightweight boots are ideal for day hikes and weekend trips, but if you intend to hike in the snow, you may find that mediumweight boots are better suited to that kind of stress.

Lightweight Boots

Lightweight boots weigh less than 2.5 pounds a pair and are generally made of a combination of leather and a "breathable" fabric. Lightweights have been around for only a decade, but it would be impossible to hike any trail without running across someone wearing a pair. Beyond the fact that they don't weigh your feet down, lightweights don't require a breaking-in period. If they do, then you're probably wearing a mediumweight boot or you've purchased the wrong size or brand.

There are disadvantages to lightweights. Your feet will get wet more quickly when it's raining or when you're walking through dew-soaked grass or leaves. On the other hand, they dry out more quickly than other boots. They offer less support than heavier boots, particularly in the ankles, and they don't last as long as heavier boots. But, taking that in account, they usually cost a lot less than heavier boots.

For all these disadvantages, lightweight boots are still the best choice for day-trips and light hiking. Still, more than half of the 2,000-milers we talked to wore lightweight boots for most of their thru-hike. It took an average of two to three pairs of lightweights to make it the 2,100-plus miles.

Although Frank lost the soles of his lightweights, it is usually the seams where the boots begin to fall apart. We know one hiker who burst the seams on four pairs of lightweights. That was an extreme, though. I wore a pair of Hi-Tec Lady Nouveaus 800 miles and am still wearing them. Separation of the boot from the sole, though less common, occurred 4 out of 14 times among the hikers we interviewed.

Most boot manufacturers offer lightweight hiking boots. Some of the more popular brands include Hi-Tec (currently the single most popular lightweight boots), Nike, Vasque, Asolo, Tecnica, New Balance and Merrell. They range in price from $45 to $100.

Mediumweight Boots
Mediumweight boots have replaced the heavyweight boots of yesterday. Weighing between 2.5 and 5 pounds per pair, medium weights are entirely, if not all, leather. They offer better ankle support and more protection in snow and cold weather. It takes them longer to get wet, and conversely, longer to dry out.

Top priority for these boots is fit. You must try them on

before you buy them, or purchase them through a mail order house with a liberal return policy. Sometimes you can get lucky. I ordered a pair of mediumweights (Raichle Ecolites) in 1985 and never had one blister. On the other hand, we met a hiker in Rainbow Springs, North Carolina, whose blisters had festered so badly, he had to seek emergency treatment in nearby Franklin. To avoid this potential problem, medium-weight boots should be broken in slowly. See the section on breaking in your boots for more information.

Make sure that the boots not only are long enough for you but also that they are wide enough. A number of boots come in several widths: find the one that's right for you.

Boots with soles that are attached with an epoxy take a bit of extra care (i.e., common sense). Don't dry them out too close to a heater because the epoxy could melt under the extreme heat–leading to, a few miles down the trail, separa-tion of the sole from the upper.

Mediumweights last longer than lightweights. Many thru-hikers found that they could hike the entire trail on a single pair of mediumweight boots, although even with these more durable boots, two pairs are often necessary. The uppers often give way before the soles. We thought, before we began our hike, that I would have to resole my mediumweights midway. Instead, the uppers gave way–seams ripped, the inside broke down, and the leather cracked. But the soles still had lots of miles left on them.

Some mediumweight boot manufacturers are Danner, Merrell, Vasque, Raichle, Fabiano, Rocky, Hermann, and the custom-made Limmers. Prices range from $100 to $150 (more than $200 for stock version of custom-made Limmers).

Heavyweight Boots
Heavyweight boots, which weigh more than 5 pounds and cost more than $250, are really not necessary for hiking anywhere on the Appalachian Trail. They are designed for

serious mountaineering, the like of which you will not encounter along the Appalachian mountain chain.

Waterproofing

If your boots have any leather in their construction, then they need waterproofing. Sno-Seal, Aquaseal and Nikwax are all popular brands of waterproofer. Devoutly follow directions for the waterproofer you purchase. It really does help to have dry feet!

Unfortunately, sealing your boots is not a one-time deal. It must be done periodically, and the more you use your boots, the more often you must seal them. For hikes of more than a week or two, you may want to carry sealant along with you. Or you may wish to send some ahead if you plan to have mail drops.

Breaking in your Boots

The single most important advice when it comes to boots is "break them in." Any experienced hiker will tell you, and it certainly cannot be stressed enough, that boots must be broken in if you intend to hike more than a mile or two in them.

Once you find a pair of boots that fit comfortably on your feet, and you have sealed them properly, then it's time to break them in. Start off by walking around your neighborhood. Wear them to the store and on short errands. If you start to get a blister, don't wait, put moleskin on it immediately. Catch a hot spot before it becomes a blister and you'll save yourself a lot of pain.

The next step is a day hike. Wear your boots for an entire day, without a pack on your back. If this goes well, you're ready for the final step. If not, continue to day-hike until the boots are comfortable. If you intend to use these boots for more than day-hiking, you may want to try hiking with a day pack to see if they are still comfortable with weight on your back. If they are, your boots need no further breaking in.

Backpacking requires more breaking in. No matter how comfortable your boots are without a pack, that could change once you add 30 or more pounds to your back. A lot of weight on your back changes the way weight is distributed over your feet. And it could change the way your feet feel in your boots. One of the strangest feelings in backpacking is taking your pack off after a long day. Suddenly, it feels as if you're walking on air. If you can backpack a good five to ten miles in your boots without creating any sore spots, your boots are ready for extensive backpacking.

Insoles

Some hikers find that they can make their boots more comfortable, and more supportive, by adding special insoles. Also, the insoles and arch supports that come with your boots begin to wear down after a while. Adding insoles that provide additional arch support can extend the life (and comfort) of your boots.

Insoles for boots can be purchased at most outfitters and department, discount and drug stores.

Carrying an Extra Pair of Shoes

Should you carry an extra pair of shoes with you when you hike?

Well, that all depends on the distance you're hiking. For day trips, you probably don't need an extra pair of shoes, especially if you're wearing lightweight boots. Weekenders must decide if they want to carry the extra weight on so short a trip. It really is a matter of preference. Some people can't stand to be in boots once they've made camp.

But if you are going to be out for more than a few days, you may wish to seriously consider additional footwear. We've seen all kinds carried—tennis shoes, espadrilles, flip flops, water socks, river shoes and sandals.

Victoria Logue watches her footing as she uses a small tree to cross a narrow, deep channel in a small stream. Boots with good gripping soles, such as the Vibram brand, are essential in situations like this one.

Photo by Frank Logue

There are a number of reasons to carry additional footwear, most of which we discovered because we didn't have anything but our boots. Picture this typical scenario. You've been hiking all day in the rain; your boots are soaked, your socks are soaked. You arrive at the shelter or campsite, make camp, and prepare to bed down. Keep in mind that this entire time you've been sloshing around in wet boots. You're no longer really moving anymore and your feet are getting cold.

Finally, you're all cuddled up in your nice, warm sleeping bag, and . . . nature calls. Do you really want to put those freezing cold, damp boots on your feet just to make a quick run into the woods?

Another example. It's a wonderful, warm, sunny day and now you have to ford a stream. There are very few times when you have the option to remove your boots and do it barefooted because of sharp rocks. On the other hand, you don't really want to get your boots wet either. A second pair of shoes is a great alternative in this case.

If you're thru-hiking, it is not unusual to wear a spare pair of shoes into town to purchase food, wash clothes, etc. And until the entire trail is moved into the woods, you may want to wear another pair of shoes on road walks. Asphalt really wears down the tread on hiking boots.

These are all good reasons to bring along a second pair of shoes. But choose wisely: the last thing you need is an extra burden.

Socks

It used to be that you needed to wear several pairs of socks with your hiking boots just to be comfortable. Fortunately, the way boots are made these days all you really need is a pair of liner socks and a pair of hiking socks.

Liners are important. They wick away the perspiration and help keep your feet dry. Liners are made of silk, nylon, polypropylene, Thermax or orlon.

Keep your liners clean. At least rinse them out often so that they don't "clog up." Socks can be hung out to dry on the back of your pack. You can use clothespins or safety pins to fasten drying clothes to the back of your pack.

Choose your outer pair of socks wisely. Most experts suggest a blend of wool and nylon or wool and polypropylene. Cotton is never suggested because, unlike wool, it will not keep you warm when it's wet.

Some socks are made with added padding at toes and heels as well as extra arch support. These socks are usually a nylon-orlon-polypropylene blend; liners are not necessary with them. Try several kinds and find out what's right for you. I discovered that mostly wool socks retained too much foot odor for my taste. Frank had absolutely no problems with his wool-polypropylene blend.

If you are having trouble keeping your feet warm when the temperature drops below freezing, try a vapor barrier. A plastic bag, such as the resealable ones used for packing food, can trap moisture and thus prevent heat from escaping. Place your socked foot into the plastic bag and then slide the bag-wrapped foot into your boot. While not fashionable, it is cozy.

◆ 8 ◆
Clothing

The type of clothing you wear will virtually determine the comfort of your hike. To use an extreme as an example, you don't want to wear wool pants and a sweater when it's 90 degrees outside. Likewise, no matter how cold the day, it doesn't take long for the exertion of hiking to heat you up.

We found ourselves in embarrassing circumstances one cold day early in our trip when we over dressed for the day's hike. We had decided we'd be smart and wear our rain pants over our underwear (instead of our long johns or pants). Surely we'd stay warm but not too warm that way.

But a couple of miles down the trail we found ourselves sweating. We didn't want to take the time to change into our shorts, so we rolled up our rain pants. Unfortunately, the slick material wouldn't stay up, it kept sliding back down our legs. In desperation, we decided to just hold them up until we stopped for lunch. Then we would change. So, there we were, marching down the trail grimly holding our pants up.

Rounding a corner, I ran, literally, into Warren Doyle, who at the time was completing his seventh hike of the Appalachian Trail. He was wearing nylon shorts. We learned our lesson. Later, we bought nylon shorts. They're light weight and stopped the rashes caused by our hipstraps. Shorts (all kinds) are often worn by hikers, even when it's cold, because the exertion of hiking generates a great deal of heat. Once you stop, it's easy enough to slip on rain pants or other warm gear.

Although clothing is undoubtedly a matter of personal preference, there are some tips that could save you a lot of frustration.

Materials

Cotton
Cotton is inefficient in the outdoors. It doesn't keep you warm when it's wet and it takes a while to dry. For this reason, clothes that might serve you well at home will not do well on a backpacking trip.

The best example of this is blue jeans. Not only are they constricting but when they get wet they double or triple in weight. They also take forever to dry. Other cotton clothing to avoid is long johns, socks, sweaters, and 100 percent cotton t-shirts.

An alternative to 100 percent cotton clothing is the cotton blends. For instance, Patagonia Baggies are made of a nylon-cotton blend and are favored by many hikers because they are lightweight, roomy and water-resistant. Patagonia makes Baggie pants and shorts. T-shirts made of cotton and a synthetic are the most popular hiking shirts because they allow freedom of movement.

For day hikes in pleasant weather and moderate altitudes, there is no reason not to wear cotton.

Wool

Wool is your best bet for winter wear, and when it is blended with polypropylene or other synthetics, it makes good socks. Wool keeps you warm when it's wet. A wool sweater can be a lifesaver on cold and/or wet days. Temperatures at high altitudes can drop below freezing even in the summer. There wasn't a state I didn't wear my sweater in even during the height of summer. If you have the pack room on an overnight summer hike, a sweater may be worth the peace of mind.

Polypropylene

This synthetic is a light weight fabric that keeps you warm when it's wet. Unlike wool, it dries out quickly. It is also non-absorbent, and when used as your first layer of clothing, it keeps your skin dry by transferring moisture to your next layer. Polypropylene is primarily used in the manufacture of long johns and socks. The only drawback to polypropylene is that it does absorb the scent of perspiration and must be washed in a specially made detergent to remove the odor.

Polypropylene must be line-dried to prevent shrinkage.

Dupont's Thermax

Thermax is another synthetic used in the manufacture of garments designed to keep you warm. Like polypropylene, it draws moisture away from your body, and its hollow-core fibers trap air, which provides insulation. Thermax can be machine washed and tumbled dry, and it does not retain the odors of perspiration.

Capilene

This polyester fiber is similar to Thermax in its attributes. It, too, resists odors and can be machine washed and dried. Both Capilene and Thermax are said to be softer than polypropylene. Capilene provides a lot of warmth for its weight.

Silk

Silk is the lightest choice for long underwear, but it tends to be less sturdy than synthetics. It gives you warmth without the bulk, and provides an effective first layer. Silk must be hand washed and line dried.

Nylon

Probably the best purchase we made while hiking was our nylon jogging shorts. Not only do they have a built-in liner (making underwear unnecessary), but they dry very quickly. The slick material also helped to keep our hip belts from rubbing us raw—a common problem.

Polar Plus and Patagonia Synchilla

These materials are good insulators. Comfortable jackets and pants in Polar Plus and Synchilla are bulky and heavy, but may be worth the extra bulk and weight on a cold night. For day hikes to higher altitudes, the insulation these materials provide offers good protection from wind and cold when you take a break. The material is too warm to actually hike in.

Clothing for Trips of One Night or More
One pair of pants*
One to two pairs of shorts
One to two short-sleeved shirts
Long-sleeved shirt
Two to three pairs of liner socks
Two to three pairs of socks
Rain gear (at least a jacket)
Long johns*
Sweater
Gloves*
Knit cap
Two pairs underwear (optional)
Bandana or two
* items optional in summer

Meister Ratte experimenting with rain gear.

Illustration by Aaron Smith

Rain Gear

"I used a rain jacket, rain pants, poncho, pack cover, and gaiters, and I still got soaked," lamented Peter Keenan.

Sometimes you're just going to get wet. Standing still in the rain, it's easy to stay dry. But once you start hiking, you increase your chances of getting wet.

Often hikers refuse to fight the battle at all in warm weather, opting to get wet by hiking in the rain in just shorts and t-shirt. That's all well and good when it's steamy outside, but what about when its cold or even just a bit chilly?

Wet clothes can lower your body temperature to the danger point. Your greatest risk of hypothermia comes when you least expect it. It doesn't have to be freezing or even near it for you to become hypothermic. A number of years ago, a hiker died of hypothermia in Georgia when he ignored his wet clothes on a 40-degree day.

Rain gear is probably one of the most essential items on your clothing checklist. There are several options in addition to the pack cover, which is mandatory (as discussed in Chapter 5).

Ponchos

Probably the least effective of all options, most backpacking ponchos are designed to cover both you and your pack. Ponchos do shield you from a lot of the rain under ideal conditions, but in the wind they are practically useless.

While a minority of hikers find ponchos meet their needs, most hikers who have tried ponchos disposed of them during their hike. Ponchos cost from $3 for a vinyl poncho to $30 for a coated nylon backpacker's poncho.

Rain Suits

Rain suits (a jacket and pants) are usually designed in sets. They can be purchased as separates, and probably afford the best protection against the cold and rain. In purchasing a rain suit, a major consideration is whether to get one in Gore-Tex or nylon.

Gore-Tex

This fabric, developed by W.L. Gore, has been adopted by a number of manufacturers of rainwear. Gore-Tex is a hotly debated subject around campfires: hikers either swear by it or swear at it.

"I chose Gore-Tex for breathability," said Ed Carlson.

"I've been using Gore-Tex because it's lightweight," said Bob Fay, "but it never really kept me dry."

"Gore-Tex is expensive but it breathes better," said Dick Hill. But Frank and I always found that we sweated to death in our Gore-tex coats; yet on really cold days, they kept us warm.

Mark Dimiceli called Gore-Tex a "monumental rip-off."

"It worked!" declared Bill and Laurie Foot of their Gore-Tex rainwear.

Victoria Logue hikes along the Appalachian Trail in Virginia during a drizzling rain.

Photo by Frank Logue

"Coated nylon is cheaper for comparable performance," Todd Gladfelter added.

Gore-Tex rain suits can be purchased in the $200 to $500 price range; most cost approximately $300. You can also purchase suits in a variety of weights—some with extra rain protection, some with liners for added warmth.

Nylon

As with Gore-Tex, coated nylon rain suits can be found in a variety of styles. Because coated nylon makes no effort to be breathable, it doesn't keep you as cool as Gore-Tex. It is also less expensive than Gore-Tex. But whether or not it is better than Gore-Tex depends on which side of the campfire you're sitting on.

Coated nylon rain suits must have the seams sealed to be effective. Seam sealer can be purchased through outfitters and mail order houses. Following the directions carefully and resealing the seams occasionally will ensure proper waterproofing.

Nylon rain suits range from about $50 to $150.

Gaiters

Hiking gaiters are made of water resistant materials; they fasten below the knee and extend to cover the upper portion of your boots. They are made to help your boots stay dry by keeping water and snow out.

Gaiters come in a variety of heights, from ankle-height to just below the knee. Some hikers wear the ankle gaiters to keep dust and leaves from working their way into their boots. Gaiters are also useful when hiking through wet brush, grass, leaves and poison ivy.

Unlike pack covers and rain suits, gaiters are not essential rainwear for any length hike. However, they may make your hikes more comfortable and are worth looking into, particularly for hikes in the snow.

Town Clothes

If you intend to spend more than a week on the trail, and especially if you're going to be long distance hiking, you may want to consider bringing along "town clothes." All this means is that you may want to stash away one t-shirt that you will wear only when hitching or hiking into a town. Your appearance, and your attitude, will determine how well you are treated and how soon you are picked up for a ride into town.

Frank and I had clean shirts set aside for these occasions (we also had shorts, which we should have left behind). We were picked up countless times by people who said they had never given a ride to a hitchhiker before!

Some female hikers carry "scrunchable" gauze skirts. They pack down small, they're light, and they're supposed to look wrinkled, anyway.

For a rough estimate of how long you have until sunset, hold your hand out at arm's length and line your fingers up with the horizon. Each finger that you can fit between the horizon and the bottom of the sun represents about 15 minutes. If six fingers separate the sun and land, the sun should set in about one-and-a-half hours.

◆ 9 ◆

Other Equipment

One evening after a tough day of hiking in Georgia, a group of hikers settled down for the night. Nestled in their sleeping bags in Gooch Gap Shelter, the hikers were suddenly disturbed by an oddly familiar sound. Nothing they had heard up to this point had prepared them for such a noise in the wild: it was the theme song from the TV show, "Jeopardy."

One of the hikers followed the sound to its source, a tent pitched by the shelter, and found that a fellow hiker, who had been complaining about his heavy pack all day, was carrying a portable television set.

In addition to the basics—tent, pack, boots, sleeping bag, etc.—there are some other articles you will probably want to bring along on a hike, especially if you're out for longer than one night. A television set isn't among them. Carefully select the equipment you really need and leave at home things that are extra, or even ridiculous. Your hike will be comfortable without the added weight, even if you have to miss your favorite game shows.

Meister Ratte, an experienced hiker, tip-toes past a heavily burdened hiker, who is presumably new to backpacking.
Illustration by Aaron Smith

Toiletries

Depending on the length of your hiking trip, you may want to consider bringing along items such as shampoo, deodorant and biodegradable soap.

Shampoo/Soap

Never, ever wash yourself or your hair in a stream, pond, or other body of water. And never use anything but biodegradable soap. Would you want to drink water that someone had rinsed soap off into? A lot of the water sources along the Appalachian Trail provide drinking water for hikers as well as animals.

Biodegradable soap (at least the widely available Dr. Bronner's) does not work as a shampoo. While you can't beat it for washing your body, it leaves your hair lank and greasy.

By the way, even the most hard-core hikers bathe occasionally.

Deodorant
Deodorant, on the other hand, is optional. We used it only on visits to a town. Otherwise there's no one around to smell you but yourself (and other smelly hikers)!

Do keep in mind, especially during the hot and humid days of summer, that you probably do reek. The longer you're out on the trail, deodorantless, the more you become accustomed to your body's odor. Which, believe it or not, isn't half as bad as the odor perspiration leaves in your clothes. They, too, ought to be washed every so often.

People will be more willing to give needy hikers a hitch if they look presentable and smell as inoffensive as possible after spending days or weeks in the woods.

Razors/Shaving cream
As for razors and shaving cream, most men opt to grow a beard when hiking, although some do take the trouble to shave every day or now and then. The same goes for women. It's all a matter of preference. I shaved at least once a week, if not more often, because I am more comfortable that way. Other women gave up shaving for the entire hike.

Toothbrush/Toothpaste
Once again, don't brush your teeth near a water source. Also, dig a small hole to spit into, and then cover your spit.

Eyecare
I was amazed at the number of hikers who elected to wear contact lenses during their four- to six-month hikes. I, too,

decided to wear contacts, although I carried a pair of glasses just in case. The new, extended wear lenses were easy to care for and the cleaning fluid did not add much weight to my pack.

I remember one night counting three out of six of us wearing contact lenses. Two wore glasses and only Frank had 20/20 vision. Improvements in hiking do not extend only to backpacking equipment!

Keep in mind that if you wear glasses, you will need to carry a baseball cap or some sort of billed hat to wear on rainy days. Otherwise, you will need windshield wipers for your glasses.

Toilet Paper

Of course you know you need to bring toilet paper. Even day hikers need it, occasionally. A good way to pack it is to scrunch it flat and stick it in a resealable plastic bag.

And, while we're on the subject. . . . One of the worst sights we saw while hiking through the Great Smoky Mountains were the wads of toilet paper scattered through the woods near shelters. Please take the time to dig a cat hole for your toilet paper, and for your feces. A backpacker's trowel weighs a mere 2 ounces. That's well worth the "trouble" when you consider how much it will lessen your environmental impact.

Never relieve yourself near a water source. Always find a site at least 50 yards downhill or to the side of a water source. This is for the protection of wildlife as well as other hikers. According to the Centers for Disease Control, beavers living downstream from national parks and forests contract giardiasis (caused by humans) more often than humans.

First-aid Kit

A few basic items should suffice for your first-aid kit. Antibiotic ointment and small adhesive bandages will help to clean and dress small cuts and scrapes. Moleskin is essential to combat blisters. A needle should be carried if the blisters need to be lanced, which should be avoided when possible. Aspirin or other pain relievers, if you use them, may help reduce hiking-induced pain, such as throbbing knees and feet. A snakebite kit isn't necessary, as discussed in Chapter 10. Anything else you may want in a first-aid kit is optional.

Lighting

Very simply put, it is a good idea to bring along some source of light for evenings at camp, shelter, or on the trail. From time to time it will be a relief to have a light to help find things in a dark tent or shelter.

Lanterns

We started out with a lantern, and continued to use ours for the entire trip, although we also bought a flashlight along the way.

The big, heavy, white gas lanterns have a place in camping but not in backpacking. They are bright and efficient, but are far too heavy and bulky to carry along on a backpacking trip.

Candle lanterns (some of which can be equipped to use gas) are your best bet if you want to carry a lantern. They weigh as little as 6 ounces. One candle will give you as much as eight hours of illumination. The light produced by a candle lantern is not that bright, but it is better than a flashlight for cooking, cleaning, reading and writing when you make camp at dark. The small flame can also help take the chill out of the air inside your tent. Be careful not to fall asleep with the candle lantern still burning.

The candle lantern is better than a candle alone because it is safer. Because it is housed in metal and glass, you are less likely to start an unwanted fire if it tips over. It is also more economical because it is protected from the wind and, thus, does not burn up as quickly as a candle. Optional light

This night scene by Mark Carroll shows the need for a flashlight.

reflectors are available that reflect the light downward, making it easier to read by in a shelter or tent.

You can purchase a candle lantern for $10 to $20 and refills for about 50 cents apiece.

Oil and gas lanterns burn for up to 20 hours per fill-up and cost about $20 to $25. They weigh the same as candle lanterns, and some can take different grades of lamp oil, including citronella (the insect repellent).

Flashlights

We didn't think we'd need a flashlight because we had a candle lantern. Even if you don't want to carry a candle lantern, you will find a flashlight very handy.

First of all, it's not easy to wake up in the middle of the night and light a candle lantern just so you don't walk into briars (or worse!) when looking for a spot to relieve yourself. Second, if you intend to hike for any length of time, don't be surprised if you end up walking at night. Whether this happens intentionally or unintentionally, you'll need a flashlight. Candle lanterns produce good light but are hard to direct.

The flashlight you take backpacking needn't be really powerful. Most hikers use the smaller flashlights equipped with two AA batteries. They are small but adequate. Mini-MagLites are popular with hikers because they provide a lot of output for very little weight. With the optional "Nite Ize" holder, you can use the light hands-free. It is a head band with a loop made to hold a Mini-MagLite securely pointed forward. Another option is the "Bite-a-Lite." It's a plastic attachment that clips onto the back of the Mini-MagLite to make it more comfortable to hold between you teeth, which is what you end up doing half the time anyway.

Flashlights that require two D cell batteries, or more, are just too heavy, and the illumination is overkill for what you'll need when hiking.

Headlamps

If you're seriously into night hiking, then you may want to purchase a headlamp. These cordless illuminators are usually on a headband and light the way ahead of you for approximately 250 feet. They are safer for night hiking because they leave your hands free. Some hikers also enjoy the convenience of reading by a headlamp at night so much, that they use one as their only flashlight.

Headlamps require two to four AA batteries and will burn for up to five hours. Popular brands include Petzl, Panasonic, and Hartford Easter Seals (sold by REI and Black Diamond). Headlamps cost about $15 to $35.

Repair Equipment

Even if you're just going out for an overnight hike, it is wise to carry along a few (small) items to help you out in a pinch. Most problems can be taken care of with these miniature repair kits.

Pack Repair

Pack pins and rings are the most frequent cause of concern. We were surprised at the number of rings we saw littering the trail from Georgia to Maine, and even more surprised when Frank's three-week-old pack lost a ring in the Shenandoahs. Rings, small circles of overlapping wire, are used to keep the pins in place on external frame packs. All those rings on the trail represented pins that were about to work their way loose from hikers' packs, causing pack bags to sag or hip belts and shoulder straps to work loose from the frame.

Carrying a couple of extra pins and rings could save you much discomfort on a hike.

Tent Repair

We were among the one-third of the hikers we spoke with who carry a tent repair kit. And boy, does it come in handy—

Meister Ratte demonstrates the need for repair equipment. The axe is not repair equipment. Carry a stove repair kit instead. The stove in this illustration by Aaron Smith is a Coleman Peak 1, which Aaron has had a lot of trouble with during his more than 3,000 miles of hiking on the A.T.

and not just for our tent. I have used it to repair my sleeping bag stuff sack, Frank's (and Craig Jolly's) rain pants as well as our tent.

Tent repair kits usually include tent fabric tape (adhesive-backed, waterproof, ripstop nylon of two types), a small amount of duct tape, a needle and thread, a short length of cord, an aluminum splint for tent poles, and no-see-um netting.

A good kit, manufactured by Outdoor Research, costs $5 and weighs only 2.5 ounces.

If you're going to be hiking more than two or three months, you'll want to send seam sealer. Extensive use is hard on a tent, and you'll need to reseal the seams every two to three months, depending on how much use your tent gets.

Stove Repair

"Carry a stove repair kit or learn how to build fires," is Phil Hall's advice.

Stoves will break or have problems when you least expect or desire it. If the manufacturer of your stove offers a kit, it is wise to purchase one. Packing the extra couple of ounces is well worth the peace of mind. We used ours, and everyone else we know of used theirs. (See Chapter 2 for more information.)

The MSR-made stoves have a reputation of being easily repaired in the field. Our experience with a Whisperlite backs that up. The Coleman Multi-fuel and Feather-series stoves have a reputation of being impossible to repair in the field, which may be undeserved. The most common problem with those stoves is a fouled preheat tube assembly, which you can replace in the field if you carry a spare. Butane stoves are not made to be repaired in the field, but they burn very cleanly and rarely need repairs anyway.

Repair kits cost approximately $5 to $10 and weigh approximately 2 ounces. Not all stove manufacturers offer repair kits for their stoves; some stoves are not designed for field repair.

Clothing Repair
At almost any drug, discount, grocery or outfitter store, you can purchase a miniature sewing kit, complete with a number of different colored threads, needle, thimble, scissors, needle threader, snaps and buttons. If you're trying to save room, you can throw an extra needle and applicable thread into your tent repair kit.

I carried an entire sewing kit (approximately two by three inches and weighing about an ounce), and used it innumerable times. Dental floss is a high-strength sewing material.

For hikes of a week or less, a sewing kit is probably unnecessary.

Boot Maintenance
Boot leather needs periodic waterproofing, and hikes of two weeks or more, particularly in wet seasons, will wear the waterproofing off your boots.

If you intend to be out for more than two weeks, you will need to either carry along Sno-Seal, Aquaseal or Nikwax or send it ahead.

Miscellaneous
There are a number of additional items that you may choose to carry on your hike, including books, journals, radios, maps and a compass. Here are three specific items—a rope (essential), a hiking stick (optional), and a gun (unnecessary).

Rope
A length of rope, at least ten feet long and approximately three-sixteenths of an inch in diameter, is absolutely necessary for hiking. Rope will definitely prove its usefulness on a hike down the A.T.

For instance, most of the Appalachian Trail is in black bear country. Whether protected or hunted, bears love human food. The Shenandoahs and the Smokies provide bearproof shelters—bear poles in the Shenandoahs and chain link fences in the Smokies. In other areas, rope can be used to tie up a bag containing your food and "smellables" to keep them out of reach of bears (see Chapter 10 for more information).

Rope's many other uses include hanging your sleeping bags to air and hanging your drying clothes.

Hiking Stick

A hiking stick can take some of the impact on the downhill and will keep you steady on rough sections of trail. If this was all they were good for, they would probably still be worth carrying. But hiking sticks also can be used to fend off stray dogs, keep your balance crossing narrow bridges or fording streams, flip small branches out of the path ahead of you, and more. Some people simply pick up a different stick every time they hike, whereas others purchase a ski pole for the purpose. Warren Doyle, who has hiked the A.T.'s length more than anyone else, swears by ski poles, noting that they are very strong, lightweight, and have a device at the tip that prevents the pole from burying itself in mud or rocks.

Firearms

Firearms are a controversial subject among hikers. Most hikers feel that guns are unnecessary, but a few do pack pistols or even rifles that break down into their packs.

Carrying weapons into a national park is a federal offense, and firearms are outlawed on other sections of trail as well. The real question is, are they necessary? To find out, we talked to hikers who collectively have hiked more than 100,000 miles on the Appalachian Trail. We decided that if the hikers we talked to could walk that far on the trail without guns being needed often, if ever, that could prove a point. The bottom line was this: there was not a single instance where a firearm was brought out of a pack (if one was carried), nor a case of a firearm helping a hiker out of a jam. None of the hikers we talked to, though some had carried guns, thought that firearms were necessary.

Guns do have a place, but the Appalachian Trail isn't it. Animals, including humans, don't present enough danger to hikers to justify carrying firearms.

Your flashlight can do double duty as a lantern. Place an empty Nalgene bottle over the flashlight and stand the bottle up on the open end. The transluscent bottle will diffuse the light and make a serviceable lantern.

◆ 10 ◆

Potential Problems

Elaine Roberts started to shiver as she stumbled toward Cold Spring Shelter on a cold, wet spring afternoon in North Carolina. It had been a long, slow climb up from Burningtown Gap, and she was relieved when she finally saw the sloping roof of the shelter.

Soaked to the skin, she sank gratefully onto the hard, wood floor of the shelter. After a few minutes, her pupils became fixed and dilated as she lapsed into unconsciousness.

On the edge of death, Elaine could do nothing to save herself.

Fortunately, the shelter was not empty when Elaine arrived. Phil Hall and seven other hikers had already arrived for the evening. Acting quickly, Phil stripped Elaine of her wet clothes and the hikers bundled her into a warm sleeping bag. An hour later, she opened her eyes to find her life had been saved by her fellow hikers.

Hypothermia

Hypothermia is a killer and claims a number of lives each year, even when the temperature is above freezing. The first signs of hypothermia—shivering, numbness, drowsiness, and marked muscular weakness—are followed by mental confusion and impairment of judgment, slurred speech, failing eyesight, and, eventually, unconsciousness. Death would have been the next step for Elaine.

Be aware of the most serious warning sign in a hypothermia victim: when the shivering stops, the victim is close to death.

You are most likely to become hypothermic when you have stopped hiking, and especially if you are tired, which is likely if you have hiked more than a few miles that day. Movement keeps you warm, but when it is chilly outside and you are wet, your body's core temperature can drop once you become still.

Fortunately, hypothermia is easy to combat. If you arrive at your campsite or shelter on a cold, wet day and are experiencing any of the symptoms mentioned above, drop everything and make yourself warm. Strip yourself of your wet clothes and put on dry clothes, if possible. Crawl into your sleeping bag, and if you're able, heat something hot to drink—tea, soup, hot chocolate—anything hot will help raise your internal temperature. Drinks with a high sugar content are best. You may want to carry a pack of fruit gelatin. It tastes great when heated and contains a lot of sugar.

Once again, remember to take hypothermia seriously. Most hypothermia victims die in 40- to 50-degree weather.

Hot Weather Ailments

The three hot weather ailments described below are serious problems and ones which can be difficult to effectively treat on a hike. The best advice is to avoid them by taking a few precautions in hot weather.

First, when you are hiking in the heat, try to maintain a consistent intake of fluids. Dehydration leads to these problems, so drinking lots of liquids will help avoid them. Second, if the heat starts to get to you, take a break. Sit down in the shade, drink some water, and give your body time to cool off.

Heat Cramps

Heat cramps are an early sign of heat exhaustion, especially if the victim is dehydrated. Cramps occur first in the muscles of the legs and abdomen. If you're experiencing heat cramps, sip salt water (one teaspoon of salt per glass), drinking 16 ounces spread out over an hour. Massaging will help relieve the cramped muscles.

Heat Exhaustion

If the heat cramps are not treated and lead to heat exhaustion, you will find that the body temperature is nearly normal. The victim's skin is pale and feels cool and clammy. It is possible that the victim will faint, but lowering his head will help him to regain consciousness. Weakness, nausea and dizziness are, in addition to cramps, symptoms of heat exhaustion. As with heat cramps, the victim needs to drink salt water. Lay the victim down, loosen his clothing, and raise his feet 8 to 12 inches. Applying cool wet cloths will also help relieve heat exhaustion.

Should the victim vomit, stop the salt water intake. At this point, medical attention should be sought.

If you experience heat exhaustion on a hike, it would be wise to take a day off or even cancel the remainder of the hike.

Heat Stroke

Treatment of heat stroke should be immediate. You will know when a hiker has heat stroke if her skin is hot, red, and dry. Her pulse will be rapid and strong, and she will probably lapse into unconsciousness.

Undress the hiker and bathe her skin with cool water or place her in a stream or other cold body of water if possible. Once her temperature lowers, dry her off. If cold water is not available, fan her with whatever you have on hand. If her temperature rises again, resume the cooling process. Never give a hiker with heat stroke stimulants, such as tea.

Once the victim's temperature begins to drop, be careful not to overchill her. This can be dangerous as the overheating she has just suffered. And, because the mortality rate associated with heat stroke is so high, medical attention should be sought as soon as the hiker is stable enough to be moved.

Burns

Early one morning in Pennsylvania's Caledonia State Park, I asked Frank for a refill on my cup of coffee. As he reached for the pot, it tipped off the stove and just-boiled water cascaded into my lap. Quick-thinking Phil Hall began dousing me with cold water and I managed to get away with only one small second degree burn on my inner thigh. Phil reacted immediately because he, too, had suffered from a similar spill that had also resulted in second degree burns.

Cook pots are susceptible to tipping and hikers are exposed to serious burns from the boiling contents as well as burns inflicted by the often relentless summer sun.

First-degree burns appear bright red. Treat these minor burns by pouring cold water over the burned area.

Second-degree burns are characterized by bright red skin, blisters and swelling. Do not break the blisters. Rather, immerse the burn in cold water or pour cold water over the burned area. Quick action will help reduce the burning effect of heat in the deeper layers of skin. Cover the burn with a sterile bandage. Antiseptic burn sprays may be used with first-degree burns but should not be used with second- or third-degree burns.

Third-degree burns are highly unlikely on a hike. These burns are distinguished by charred flesh and must be treated in a hospital. If third-degree burns occur, do not remove clothing, which may adhere to the burns. If you cannot get to a hospital within an hour, give the victim salt water. Unlike first- and second-degree burns, do not immerse the burn in cold water. Cover the area with a clean cloth and get the victim to a doctor immediately.

Blisters

Blisters heal slowly if you continue to hike and keep them aggravated. The best way to avoid this problem is to treat blisters before they occur.

When a part of your foot feels hot or tender, stop hiking. Take your shoes and socks off and inspect the tender area. Cut out a piece of moleskin that is larger than the "hot spot" that you will be covering. Apply the moleskin to the hot spot and put your socks and boots back on. Quick action at this stage may prevent blisters all together.

If you do get a blister, try to leave the blister unbroken. If it is still small and relatively flat, cover the blister with moleskin and resume hiking. Should the blister get worse, wash the area with soap and water, and then, with a sterilized needle (hold in a flame until the tip turns red), make a small hole in the bottom of the blister so that the fluid drains. Once the blister is drained, apply a sterile bandage to prevent further irritation and infection.

If the blister is already broken, treat it like an open wound (cleanse and bandage it), and watch for signs of infection. If necessary, quit hiking for a day or two and let your blisters heal.

Shin Splints, Tendonitis, and Other Hiking-related Problems

Extreme pain, and often swelling, characterize hiking-related problems in the knees, shins, ankles and feet. Taking a day or two off often will relieve the problem, but should the pain continue (or the swelling increase), only a doctor can tell you if your problem requires medical treatment.

It is not unusual for a hiker to experience some sort of pain every day he is on the trail. As one thru-hiker put it: if the pain moves around, you're probably all right. But if it remains in one place, then it is more than likely something serious. Don't wait to see a doctor if there is swelling and continual pain. Nothing is worth causing permanent damage to your body. The doctor probably will prescribe an anti-inflammatory and a week or more off your feet.

Even if you're hiking the entire trail, it's not the end of the world. Frank had shin splints and was forced to take a week off. We still managed to complete the trail in six months–five months of hiking and a month off for various reasons, including shin splints, a wedding and a graduation. But had he not seen a doctor, he could have caused permanent damage to his calves, including gangrene.

Knee Problems

One of the most common complaints is of knee pain. Fortunately, the tenderness in the joints doesn't necessarily signal a problem. Aspirin or other pain relievers can help alleviate some of the pain. Wearing a knee brace can help prevent knee problems or aid in support once a problem develops. If you have a history of knee problems, it is good idea to carry a brace, just in case.

Wildlife

Lions and tigers and bears, oh my!

Dorothy, Scarecrow, Tin Man and the Cowardly Lion repeated the chant over and over as they followed the yellow-brick road toward Oz. In the movie, their fears of the woods were justified, but on the Appalachian Trail, animals don't present a real threat to hikers.

A little caution and courtesy toward animals will go a long way. The following are among the animals that hikers are likely to meet while hiking on the Appalachian Trail.

Bears

The Black Bear has a commanding presence and can summon an ominous "woof" to warn backpackers to stay away, but a face-to-face encounter will probably end with the bear ambling, if not scurrying, away.

"I was walking along the trail and I saw three bears–a mother bear and two cubs," Doug Davis said, remembering an encounter with bears in the Shenandoahs. "Evidently, they heard a car approaching and they headed my way to move away from the vehicle and went toward the edge of a ledge. At that time, I was coming up the trail and saw the bears. When they saw me, the mother and one cub began running away from me."

One of the cubs, however, rolled down the ledge toward Davis, landing at his feet. But he hiked on without hearing even a snort of protest from the mother bear who is usually very protective of her young.

Davis got closer to a bear than most hikers, who usually see them from a distance. The National Park Service offers some tips on how to handle bear encounters as well as how to prevent them from getting into your food and pack. The following discussion is based on those recommendations.

Bears are hunted in national forests and, thus, are usually wary of humans there; but in national parks, bears can be conniving when it comes to looking for food.

If you stop to take a break in bear country, keep your pack nearby. If a bear approaches, throw your pack on, pick up whatever you have out, and leave the area. Bears have been known to bluff hikers into leaving food behind. Don't fall for this ploy, but, on the other hand, don't take your time getting out either. Avoid trouble at all costs. Bears seldom attack, but when they do, they can do plenty of damage.

Should a bear charge you, by all means don't run. Like many animals, bears react to running as if it is "food" trying to escape them. Don't bother trying to climb a tree, either;

bears are adept at climbing trees, and can probably do so faster and better than you can. They also can outrun you. Your best bet is to lie on the ground in the fetal position, arms drawn up to protect your face and neck. Most bears will leave you alone if you do this or content themselves with a scratch or two. Also, never, ever look a bear (or any animal) in the eye. Direct eye contact is perceived as aggressive.

Never, under any circumstances, try to feed a bear or leave food to attract them. Once a bear has tasted human food, he will continue to search for it, which means trouble for the bear as well as humans.

When making camp for the night, stash your food in a bag and make sure it is securely tied off the ground and between two trees. The bag should be approximately ten feet off the ground and ten feet from the nearest tree.

In the two areas that see the most bears—the Smokies and the Shenandoahs—bearproof means of storage are provided for hikers. In the Smokies, chain-link fences are supposed to keep bears from getting into shelters (although bears have been known to keep humans from getting into the shelters when the door in the fence has been left open). In the Shenandoahs, the park service provides bear poles—tall, metal poles with four prongs at the top from which food bags can be suspended. A gaff is provided.

Snakes

In the wild, snakes lie in wait along a path for small rodents or other prey. Coiled along the edge of a trail waiting for food to pass by, the patient reptiles test the air with their flicking tongues for signs of game.

This image of the snake lying in wait just off the trail is a cause of concern among some hikers; but what about the snake's view of things? The snake is aware of its place in the food chain; it must watch for predators as well as prey. A hiker making a moderate amount of noise will usually be perceived as a predator and the snake will back off or lie still until the "danger" passes.

Garter snakes, ribbon snakes and black rat snakes are among the nonpoisonous snakes commonly found in the Appalachian mountains. Rattlesnakes and copperheads are the only species of poisonous snake you could possibly encounter on the Appalachian Trail. Both the rattlesnake and copperhead are not aggressive and will avoid striking a human unless cornered.

To avoid confrontations with snakes, remember to make a little extra noise when you are walking through brush, deep grass, or piles of dead leaves that block your view of the footpath. This will warn snakes of your approach. By kicking at the brush or leaves slightly, you will make enough noise to cause a snake to slither off or lie still.

Both species of poisonous snake prefer areas near rocky outcrops, and copperheads can be found among the boulders that border rocky streams as well. Viewpoints, such as Zeager Cliffs in Pennsylvania, are popular sunning spots for snakes. Poisonous snakes do not occur as far north as Maine, and copperheads do not commonly appear in Vermont and New Hampshire. Here are some tips for recognizing these two poisonous snakes.

Copperheads

Copperheads are typically two to three feet in length. They have moderately stout-bodies with brown or chestnut hourglass-shaped crossbands. The background color is lighter than the crossbands, anything from reddish brown to chestnut, to gray-brown. The margins of the crossbands have a darker outline. This pattern certainly helps the copperhead blend in among dead leaves. Other, nonpoisonous snakes (e.g., corn snake) have similar markings, but none are so distinctively hourglass-shaped.

Copperheads prefer companionship; if you see one copperhead, there are probably others in the area. In the spring and fall they can be seen in groups, particularly in rocky areas.

Copperheads avoid trouble by lying still and will quickly retreat as a last resort. The bite of a copperhead is almost never fatal. Rarely has someone weighing more than 40 pounds died of a copperhead bite. Its bite produces discoloration, massive swelling and severe pain. While not fatal, the bite is dangerous and medical attention should be sought immediately.

Rattlesnakes

Rattlesnakes are heavy-bodied and can be anywhere from three to five feet long, though large rattlesnakes are increasingly rare. Rattlesnakes also have dark blotches and crossbands (though these are not hourglass-shaped). There are two color phases (i.e., the background color)–a yellowish and a dark, almost black one. Sometimes their overall color is dark enough to obscure the pattern. A real giveaway is the prominent rattle or enlarged "button" on the end of the tail. Rattlesnakes usually warn predators with a distinctive rattle; but this can't be relied on because they may also lie still while hikers go by.

Because of the rattlesnake's size, its bite is more serious than that of the copperhead. But like the copperhead, it will strike only as a last resort.

Rattlesnakes are frequently seen on the trail, though their presence has been greatly reduced by development encroaching on their terrain. Cases of rattlesnake bites are almost unheard of and when quick action is taken, they will almost never prove fatal, except among the very young or very old.

Treating Nonpoisonous Snakebites

By making a little extra noise in areas where snakes may be hidden from view, you should avoid any chance of snakebite. If a bite should occur, proper treatment is important.

The bite of a nonpoisonous snake can be dangerous. If not properly cleaned, the wound can become infected. Ideally, the victim should be treated with a tetanus shot to prevent serious infection. Nonpoisonous snake bites will cause a moderate amount of swelling. If large amounts of swelling take place, the bite should be treated as if it were caused by a poisonous snake.

Treating Poisonous Snakebites

The reaction to the bite of a poisonous snake will be swift. Discoloration and swelling of the bite area are the most visible signs. Weakness and rapid pulse are other symptoms. Nausea, vomiting, fading vision, and shock also are possible signs of a poisonous bite and may develop in the first hour or so after being bitten.

It is important to know that tourniquets can cause more damage to the victim than a snakebite. If improperly applied, the tourniquet can cause the death of the infected limb and the need for amputation. The cutting and suction methods called for in snakebite kits also are not recommended.

The best treatment is to reduce the amount of circulation in the area where the bite occurred and seek medical attention immediately. Circulation can be reduced by keeping the victim immobile (which isn't easy if the bite occurs five miles from the nearest road); by applying a cold, wet cloth to the area; or by using a constricting band. A constricting band is not a tourniquet and should be tight enough only to stop surface flow of blood and decrease the flow of lymph from the wound. The constricting band should not stop blood flow to the limb.

Boars

Boars, which are not indigenous to the United States (they were brought here from Europe for hunting purposes), can be found in the Southern Appalachians, especially in Great Smoky Mountains National Park. They are rarely seen, and like most animals, will disappear if they hear you coming.

Should you happen upon a boar, try to avoid direct confrontation; just continue hiking.

Shelter Pests

Appalachian Trail shelters attract rodents and other small mammals. These creatures are searching for food and can do much damage, especially if you do not take care to protect your belongings.

It is never wise, even when camping along the Appalachian Trail, to leave your pack, and particularly, your food, out on the ground or shelter floor for the night. Food, and sometimes whole packs, should be hung where these animals cannot reach them.

Porcupines

These nocturnal creatures are shelter pests in the New England states. They love to gnaw on outhouses and shelters, and are particularly fond of hiking boots and backpack shoulder straps. That may sound strange, but they are after the salt from your sweat. So hang your packs and boots when you're hiking in New England, and take particular care in shelters that are known to be frequented by porcupines. Fortunately, most of the shelters have been porcupine-proofed: metal strips have been placed along the edges of the shelters to prevent the rodents from chewing on it.

Direct contact is necessary to receive the brunt of the porcupine's quills. Although it is unlikely for a hiker to be lashed by a porcupine's tail, it is not unusual for a dog to provoke a porcupine into defending itself.

Animals, like the bears and squirrel in this illustration by Mark Carroll, can be very clever when it comes to getting into your food supply.

Porcupine quills become embedded in the flesh of the attacker, causing extreme pain. If the quills are not removed immediately, they can cause death.

Skunks

Skunks inhabit the entire length of the trail but are really only a problem for hikers in the Smokies. Dogs, on the other hand, can provoke skunk attacks from Georgia to Maine. Although we only saw skunks in the Smokies, we were aware of their presence (that telltale odor!) our entire trip.

During our night at Ice Water Springs Shelter north of Newfound Gap in the Smokies, a brazen skunk wove around our legs as we warmed ourselves in front of the campfire. It was very pleasant, scrounging for scraps of food on the shelter's dirt floor and along the wire bunks. The skunk occasionally stood on its hind legs and made a begging motion, which had no doubt been perfected on earlier hikers. We didn't give in to the skunk's pleas for food, and it eventually crawled back up under the bunks as we sighed in relief.

We heard of another skunk encounter in the same shelter, perhaps with the same skunk, a year earlier, when two British hikers, who were unfamiliar with the animal, tried to chase the skunk away by throwing a boot. They were given a quick course in skunk etiquette!

Mice

Mice are the most common pests to be found in shelters. It doesn't take long after a new shelter has been built for the mice to move in. They faithfully clean the shelter of even the smallest scraps of food. At night they perform acrobatics along the beams of the shelter as they climb around after packs hung from the ceiling or on the walls of the shelter.

If you leave your pack sitting on the floor of a shelter, plan on the mice gnawing their way into your food bags and helping themselves to a mouse-sized portion of your food or clothes. While we were hiking in Virginia, I decided to change into a warmer shirt mid-morning, and was shocked to find that mice had gnawed several holes in the shirt's collar.

A few hikers carry along mousetraps, but this is a little controversial: some hikers feel that the mice have a place in the "shelter ecosystem."

Dogs

Some dogs encountered on the trail are hiking companions and others are strays or property of people who live along the trail's route. They can be very friendly as well as hard to get rid of when they are strays. They can also be aggressive, especially if they feel they are defending their territory or their masters.

Fortunately, most of the dogs you meet on the A.T. are friendly. While hiking over The Humps (Tennessee) in the aftermath of a snowstorm, we were forced to contend with high winds and limited visibility as well as snow that ranged in depth from two inches to three-foot drifts. A stray dog had appeared at the shelter the previous night, and joined us when we set out for the eight-mile trip to town that morning.

As we climbed blindly over the wind-blown balds, the dog unerringly led us along the Appalachian Trail. At one point, a road very clearly led straight ahead while the trail turned off to the left. We did not notice the trail's turning, but the dog did. He turned left and we followed. Soon we saw blazes at the edge of the woods. Several times during that eight-hour hike, the dog kept us from wandering off the trail and into the woods when the trail's white-blazed trees were hidden beneath snow that had stuck to the trunks.

We also had bad experiences with dogs. In Vermont, a huge Newfoundland stood on its hind legs, barely two inches from my face, and growled, menacingly, his teeth bared. The tactic was apparently a very frightening bluff, which left me (and many other hikers) shaking. Stories of this particular dog filled the register at the next shelter.

How to Avoid Troublesome Dogs

As with bears and most other animals, don't run. Don't look directly into a dog's eyes, but if it is necessary to defend yourself, use your hiking stick or small stones. Sometimes just picking up a stone and holding it as if you're going to throw it is enough to dissuade a dog. Throw the rock only if it's absolutely necessary.

Dogs as Hiking Partners

Although dogs can make wonderful hiking partners, most hikers we interviewed said they really prefer not to hike around people who are hiking with dogs.

Unless you have complete control over your animal, you are probably going to make a lot of people unhappy, especially if you intend to stay in a shelter. Two of the biggest complaints from hikers were about wet dogs climbing all over their sleeping bags and other gear, and dogs who tried to eat their food.

Peter Keenan had a positive experience with his dog, Bobo, even though other hikers had occasional complaints. Bobo, who started hiking the trail as a puppy, only knew about life on the trail. She had a way of lifting up spirits on cold and wet days with her boundless energy, and she was always ready for a game of fetch–even after a 20-mile day. We mention this only because there are two ways of looking at hiking with dogs. Obviously, things are going to be a lot different if the dog is your hiking partner: you'll probably be indifferent to your wet dog lying on your sleeping bag or your hungry dog begging for your food.

Keep in mind, if you plan to take a dog, that dogs usually are not welcomed by other hikers and do not have priority when it comes to shelter space. Dogs also are not allowed in the Smokies or in Baxter State Park and, therefore, cannot even legally complete a thru-hike.

Dogs also tend to scare up trouble. One hiker's dog was rattlesnake-bit in Virginia, and an expensive treatment was necessary to save the dog. Also, if you choose to hike with a dog, you probably won't see much wildlife.

If you do bring a dog on the trail, make sure you keep it under control. We were chased by some dogs in New Hampshire who, a few minutes later, bit another hiker. The dogs were on a day hike with their owners.

Other reasons not to bring a dog include the rough rock scrambling in several states and the intense heat of summer. We witnessed the death of a dog who had overheated in 90-plus-degree weather on a day hike in Pennsylvania. The owner, though well-intentioned, had neglected to bring enough water for his pet. Consider the kindness of leaving your dog at home, especially when you intend to thru-hike.

Problem People

In 1990 the murders of Geoff Hood and Molly LaRue in a Pennsylvania shelter sent shock waves through the hiking community. Even the nation felt the impact of their untimely and violent deaths as national news picked up the story. How could something like that happen in the wilderness?

Unfortunately, this is not the first time such a tragedy has occurred on the Appalachian Trail. It is doubtful it will be the last. Although the number of murders in its 50-plus-year history are few (six), the Appalachian Trail, situated along the highly-populated eastern seaboard, is not immune from problems involving humans. Rapes, thefts and general harrassment are also reported.

Why? Because where there are humans there are problems. Even after the arrest and conviction of Paul David Crews for the murders of Geoff and Molly, hikers could still not shake the feeling of "will it happen to me?" Your safety, on the Appalachian or any trail, cannot be guaranteed. But following these guidelines will help:

- Avoid camping near road crossings or staying in shelters within a mile of a road crossing.
- Do not tell strangers exactly where you intend to camp for the night.
- If you get a funny feeling about someone sharing a campsite or shelter with you, move on no matter how late it is or how tired you are.
- Take any valuables (e.g., wallet) with you; do not leave anything of any worth in your car at the trailhead.
- Hiking with others does not ensure your safety. A couple should be as wary a solo hiker.
- If something does happen, report it to local law authorities (and the Appalachian Trail Conference) no matter how insignificant it may seem. It may be part of a bigger picture that you are unaware of.

If your pack is not in your tent with you, leave the pack pockets open at night. Mice, chipmunks and other rodents have a way of finding packs, particularly at frequently used campsites. If the pockets are open, rodents won't have to chew their way into your pack to search for food.

◆ 11 ◆
Preparing for Your First Hike

The best advice, when it comes to your first hike, is: Don't bite off more than you can chew. It is very easy to run yourself into the ground, and it takes a lot longer to hike ten rugged miles than you would think.

A lot of people assume that a four-mile-an-hour pace is standard. Well, it is if you're walking around a track or on a level stretch of road. But even the most seasoned hiker finds it next to impossible to keep a four-mile-an-hour pace on tough terrain. A two- to three-mile-an-hour pace is average for a hiker in peak condition.

How Far and How Fast?
Don't plan on more than ten miles a day when you first start hiking. A five-mile day hike is a good choice. It will allow you plenty of time to enjoy the scenery without overextending yourself.

For an overnight hike, plan on a 10- to 20-mile, two-day

trip. After several smaller hikes, you may decide that you can extend your backpacking trips without ruining the fun of them.

You don't have to be in great shape to backpack. But if you're not in good shape, you should allow yourself time to adjust.

Phil Hall had a novel idea for training for his first hike: "I carried around a 70-pound bag of birdseed on my shoulders for ten miles over a ten-day period," he said. "From this, I got a tired and sore neck but discovered a clever way of hitching rides, easily."

Phil realized the folly of his plan, chucked the bag of birdseed and took the direct approach.

"I then decided that I would just start out slowly and do however many miles I could." He had the right idea. The only way to adjust to backpacking is to backpack. Unfortunately, there is no other way to prepare yourself. Being in good cardiovascular condition helps, but it takes the body time to accustom itself to the strain of even a light pack.

When you first start hiking, don't count on more than a one-mile-per-hour pace with a full pack. Allow yourself ten hours to hike ten miles. Your actual walking pace will probably be faster, but your body will crave frequent breaks.

It won't take long before you can easily walk two miles per hour. A good rule of thumb for planning your trip is to allow an hour for every two miles of trail plus one hour for each one thousand feet of elevation to be gained. So, for a hike that will cover 14 miles and have an elevation gain totaling 3000 feet, you should allow yourself ten hours.

Taking Breaks

When we first started hiking, we took what we called a pack-off break every two miles and pack-on breaks after almost every hill. A pack-on or bend-over break is accomplished by leaning over and holding your knees so that your back supports all the pack's weight. Try it; it really helps when you first start hiking. By the time we had hiked 500 miles, we could hike for hours without any breaks at all.

Taking breaks does slow down your overall pace. One way to avoid frequent stops is to use the rest step when ascending mountains. Perform the rest step by pausing for a moment with all your weight centered on your downhill leg, which should be kept straight. Then step forward and pause again with your weight on the opposite leg, which is now the downhill leg. Vary the length of the pause as needed. This step will not only get you up a steep slope sooner but will get you up a mountain with less effort.

The idea is to use this step on extremely tough sections of a hike by pausing slightly with each step—continual movement instead of vigorous hiking separated by a number of breaks.

Minimize Your Impact

In recent years "minimum impact camping" has become the catchphrase for responsible outdoors behavior. Groups, such as the Boy Scouts, who once espoused techniques like trenching around your tent to prevent water from running under it, have adopted low-impact techniques.

Minimum impact camping is a philosophy once summed up by the National Park Service as "Take nothing but pictures, leave nothing but footprints."

The following are measures you can, and should, take to eliminate any trace of your presence along the trail.

- Carry out all of your trash
- Carry out trash left by others, when possible
- Cook on a stove rather than fires
- Limit your group size to ten or less
- Stay on the designated trail (don't cut switchbacks)
- Camp in designated sites or well away from the trail

Steve Marsh's guide to trail etiquette.

- Don't use soap in or near streams
- Pack out organic trash or scatter it well away from the trail (an orange peel takes up to five months to rot)
- If you build a fire, do not burn or leave trash in the pit
- Use only downed wood for fires
- Build fires only in designated fire pits
- Do not try to burn tinfoil-lined packages in fire pits; pack them out

This is not a list of rules; it is a way of living that is becoming increasingly important to adopt. About four million people hike some portion of the Appalachian Trail annually. If these techniques are not used by everyone (and currently they're not), the trail will lose its natural beauty. Nature is reslient but its ability to fight back is limited. It takes a long time for a campsite to recover from a single overnight stay by an inconsiderate group of hikers.

When you leave a campsite, take a long, hard look at it. It should look better than when you found it. And if you camp off the trail, it should look as if you had never been there. It can be done. We've even gone so far as to rescatter leaves and fluff up grass so that you could not tell that our tent had been pitched there. It only takes a few minutes and your efforts are more than compensated for with peace of mind.

Where Permits Are Needed and How to Get Them

Permits are needed only within the national park system, and in the case of the Appalachian Trail, in the Smokies and the Shenandoahs. The heavy use of the A.T. in these areas has created a need to limit the number of hikers staying overnight in the parks. The permits are free and are used only to control the number of campers.

Great Smoky Mountains National Park (GSMNP)
The backcountry reservation office is open daily from 8 A.M.

to 6 P.M. The telephone number is (615) 436-1231. You will need to plan your intinerary before you call so that you can notify them of exactly which site(s) you intend to occupy on which night(s). You are limited to no more than one consecutive night per shelter. Hiking without a permit in the Smokies can result in a fine and ejection from the park.

If you are thru-hiking, you can self-register at both Fontana Dam and Davenport Gap, the southern and northern entrances to the park. GSMNP considers anyone starting more than 50 miles out of the park and ending their hike more than 50 miles on the other side of the park a thru-hiker.

Shenandoah National Park (SNP)
Permits for backcountry camping in the Shenandoahs can be obtained at the park entrance stations, campgrounds, and visitors centers in the park. There is a $10 entrance fee to drive into the park but this fee is waived if you obtain a backcountry permit at an entrance gate.

Should you desire to make reservations, SNP requires that you write for them at least two weeks in advance at Shenandoah National Park, Route 4, Box 348, Luray, Virginia 22835.

Other Reservations
Reservations are also required if you plan to stay at the Appalachian Mountain Club huts in the White Mountains of New Hampshire. (There is a fee for staying in the huts, which is discussed in Chapter 4.) There is also a new fee (as of 1997) of $5 per week for unattended cars. A $20 annual pass is also available. Write AMC Pinkham Notch Camp, P.O. Box 298, Gorham, New Hampshire 03581; or call (603) 466-2727.

Guidebooks
The Appalachian Trail Conference offers a number of books that can help you with planning and carrying out a hike.

The Appalachian Trail Guidebook Series
This series of 11 books offers detailed trail descriptions for both north-to-south and south-to-north hikes. The books provide information on mileage between major points, shelters and facilities on the trail, road crossings and trailhead parking, water, side trails, and relevant history of the area the trail is passing through.

All of the guidebooks come with 3 to 12 maps as well. The topographic maps also include elevation profiles, which should not be taken literally: flat sections on the elevation profile are almost never truly level when you are actually hiking the trail. And some steep sections, especially those on the Maine maps, are not quite as bad as they appear on the profile.

These books, while helpful in deciding where to go and how to get there, are not essential for the actual hike. The Appalachian Trail is well-blazed, and a detailed, step-by-step description is not necessary to keep from getting lost. The trail descriptions do, however, keep you informed of your progress and how far it is to the next shelter, water, etc.

The guidebooks also can be frustrating. An extreme case is that of a hiker we heard about who checked off every feature in his guidebook as he hiked. This caused him to curse the book repeatedly when he found a section to be steep that was described as moderate, or when he arrived at the site of a spring mentioned in the guidebook, which was no longer flowing.

Guidebooks cannot be taken as Gospel. The trail route is altered, storms knock down trees, springs dry up and appear, and the trail descriptions are the opinions of the writer.

The guides are updated every couple of years or so. They can be purchased together with the maps or you can buy the maps separately.

Data Book

The *Appalachian Trail Data Book* is updated annually to keep current with the relocations of the trail. It contains mileages between points on the trail. At road crossings, the *Data Book* lists distances to post offices, lodgings, groceries and restaurants.

This book informs you of the location of shelters and notes if the shelter doesn't have water available. It also lets you know the distance between sources of water in water scarce areas.

The ATC intended the *Data Book* to be used only for broad scale planning of hikes; but it is also a practical guide that can be taken along with you (or a photocopy of the pages you need), particularly if you opt not to carry the trail guidebooks. See Appendix 2 for more books about the A.T.

Finding Solitude

Many hikers retreat to the Appalachian Trail seeking a wilderness experience, only to find themselves on a crowded section of trail sharing their "wilderness experience" with more hikers than they bargained for. Here are a few tips for finding a little solitude on America's most popular long-distance trail.

Start your hike early in the morning. We once took this advice to the extreme and enjoyed the best hike of our lives for the effort. We started climbing Katahdin at 2:30 A.M. and were up at Baxter Peak by 5:30 A.M. for the sunrise. The view was spectacular, and the three of us hiking together didn't share the summit with another hiker. That was on Labor Day weekend, when later in the day hikers marched in a long single file line from Baxter Peak to Pamola Peak. By making an extra effort to get up early (and hike the tricky section of trail in the dark), we had the peak to ourselves on perhaps the busiest day of the year.

Another way to find your own piece of the A.T. is to go

Mark Carroll shows a hiker sorting out–or trying to, anyway–directions from his maps, Data Book *and the now-out-of-print* Philosopher's Guide.

during the off-season. Roan Highlands on the Tennessee/ North Carolina state line is very crowded during the peak bloom time for the rhododendron garden. Visitors flock to see the awesome spectacle of thousands of big catawba rhododendrons in bloom at once. But we have camped alone on the summit during the winter. We couldn't see the rhododendron blooms that attract the big crowds, but the mountain covered in fresh snow was a magnificent sight, and we didn't have to share it with hoards of hikers.

The third way to find solitude on the country's most popular long distance trail is to find your own special places. There are a number of very popular areas on the A.T. from Blood Mountain in Georgia and Shenandoah National Park in Virginia to Katahdin in Maine as well as many others. Most of the use of the trail is concentrated in these easy-to-access spots, while many other areas go unappreciated. Join a trail club in your area and learn from other members and group hikes where some of the less visited areas are.

Hiking downhill is as tough on your body as an uphill climb. Whereas an ascent places cardiovascular stress on your body, a descent takes its toll on your feet and knees. To lessen the impact try pausing with your weight on one foot between each step; this will relieve some of the strain. Also, spring forward with each step, flexing your legs as you put weight on them. This is the fastest and safest way to get downhill.

◆ 12 ◆
Winter Backpacking

Snows in Georgia are rare, so when Frank and I heard that the North Georgia mountains were going to receive several inches of snow, we planned an impromptu dayhike. We piled into our Jeep with our friends, Joe and Monica Cook, and our daughter, Griffin, and headed for the hills.

In four-wheel drive, we labored up the forest service road to the base of Springer Moutain, the southern terminus of the Appalachian Trail. Seeing your favorite spots encrusted and powdered with snow is like walking in an entirely different world. Thrilled with the first hike, we headed down to Three Forks to see what kind of fairy kingdom the snow had made down there. It was an idyllic scene. Noontootla Creek burbled along as if it were an ordinary day, but the rhododendron on its banks were frosted with an icing of snow, and even the exposed stones in the creek boasted an inch or two of powder.

Experienced hikers have learned that pleasurable hiking

Noontootla Creek, on the A.T. in Georgia, is bordered by rhodo-dendrons blanketed in snow.

Photo by Victoria Logue

need not only be found during the spring, summer and fall. Winter camping is possible in many parts of the U.S. and provides much more solitude. It is a way to experience the Earth during its darkest season—to discover a new world both physically and mentally.

Even in the south, where contrary to popular opinion, it does get cold and even has the occasional snow, you'll find the trails much less crowded. By the same token, you can find snowy places throughout the country where you can hike and camp in peace.

Before you throw on your pack and snow-seal your boots, keep in mind that winter backpacking requires a little more forethought as well as preparation.

First, you must decide whether you intend to hike in boots (with or without crampons), on snowshoes or on cross-country skis. If the snow is not deep or if it is hard-packed, boots will probably suffice. A pair of gaiters and well-sealed boots will make the trip more comfortable. The hard, plastic, cold-weather, mountaineering boots which were designed for technical climbing are impractical for backpacking.

If you plan a trip in snow that will be knee-deep or more, you will want to opt for snow shoes or cross-country skis to get you to your destination.

Crampons and Snowshoes

Some backpacking requires the use of crampons. Simply put, crampons are used for hiking on ice and hard snow. While not necessary for most backpacking trips, there are areas along the A.T. where they are essential in winter.

Crampons, usually twelve-pointed, strap onto your boots. They must be fitted properly—loose crampons can be more dangerous than hiking crampon-less across slick ice or snow. For backpacking, flexible crampons are a must. Consult an outdoors store that features climbing equipment when choosing a pair of crampons.

When hiking with crampons, an ice ax is another useful piece of equipment. It will help you cut steps in ice or snow and can be used as a brake to stop yourself should you fall. The purchase of an ice ax should be discussed with your local outfitter.

If you're going to be doing a lot of backpacking in soft snow—the kind you can sink up to your waist in—it would be wise to look into purchasing a pair of snowshoes. Remember though, that even with snowshoes, four hours a day is about all most people can manage to backpack in the snow.

The traditional snowshoes of wood and rawhide are still available but are giving way to technologically superior frames of aluminum and thongs of nylon and plastic. A good pair can be purchased for approximately $150.

When purchasing snowshoes, there are five qualities you should look for:

1) Flotation—the surface area of the snowshoe. A back-

packer will need more surface area because of the added weight of his pack. The greater the surface area, the more weight a snowshoe can support. But keep in mind that firm snow or packed trails will also support more weight than powder. Purchase snowshoes based on the conditions you will likely be hiking in as well as the weight to be supported (the combined weight of the hiker and pack).

2) Traction—depending on how much climbing you will do, your snowshoe will need more traction. An optional climbing crampon can help you gain more traction for rugged, mountainous sections of trail.

3) Tracking ability—the shoe should be heavier in the tail than in the toe, and your boot toe should fit through the toe hole and dig into the snow.

4) Traversing ability—a narrow design of ten inches or less is best. Wider designs are too unwieldy.

5) Weight—the lighter they are the better. There is an old saying that "a pound on the foot is equal to five on the back." That is very close to the truth. Aluminum alloy frames combined with neoprene, Polyurethane or Quadex decking have helped to reduce snowshoe weight in recent years.

When it comes to purchasing snowshoes, there are five basic designs to choose from: 1) Green Mountain Bearpaw, for mountainous, wooded terrain; 2) Cross Country, similar to the Bearpaw but with a ten-inch tail; 3) Michigan, for trail and sparse-forest travel; 4) Alaskan, for open country and deep snow; and 5) Ojibwa, similar to the Alaskan—for open country and deep snow.

Sorel, or other insulated boots, are worn with snowshoes to keep your feet dry and warm.

A pair of ski poles can be of assistance in snowshoeing as well as skiing (many backpackers use ski poles as hiking sticks as well. A good book on the subject is *Snowshoeing* by Gene Prater (published by The Mountaineers).

Other Winter Equipment

Tent

After you determine your method of transportation, you will need to load your pack. If you're heading out into the snow, you'll need a four-season tent, preferably one that offers a cook hole in its floor. In the deep South, a three-season tent will probably suffice at all but the highest altitudes, since the temperature rarely drops below 20 degrees Fahrenheit.

A freestanding, four-season tent is the best choice for snow camping. Non-freestanding tents need special pegs to keep the tent anchored in the snow and even these don't always work, but a freestanding tent doesn't need to be anchored except in very strong winds. You will also need a tent with a waterproof floor.

Some four-season tents offer cookholes: a zippered or gathered hole in the bottom of the tent floor that can be flapped or pulled back so that you may cook directly on the ground. A cookhole is preferable to cooking on the floor of your tent, which can catch fire easily should the stove tip. Fumes and the danger of starting a fire are potential problems. You should only cook in the tent itself if weather dictates. Cooking in the vestibule is generally a safer option.

When pitching your tent in the snow, make sure you level the area and pack the snow down. If this is not done, it is very likely you will wake up when the tent collapses on your head. Leaving your pack on while you stamp the ground flat will give you some extra weight that will make the job go more quickly. If you make the base wider than necessary, you'll be able to walk around your tent without snowshoes or skis, especially useful should nature call in the middle of the night.

Special tent pegs for snow camping can be purchased from most outdoors stores. Once your tent is pegged, try pouring some water on the pegs. Once it freezes, the pegs really won't move.

Sleeping Bag

When camping during the winter, you will also need a sleeping bag with a low comfort rating—a zero-degree bag will do for most situations. If you don't want the expense of two sleeping bags, consider using a liner to make your three-season bag warmer. It should go without saying that you will need a mummy-style bag for winter camping. Mummy bags fit more closely to your body than square-cut bags, offering better insulating ability. Also, with less cold air coming into the open end of the bag, the mummy bags keep you warmer. If the temperature really drops, you can tighten the hood until nothing but your nose is showing. Some sleeping bags are available with extra insulation in the foot of the bag to combat cold feet.

Since the bottom of your tent may be on top of snow, you will want some good insulation between the bottom of your tent and yourself. While a three-quarter sleeping pad may do for three-season camping, if your feet get cold easily you may want to consider a full-length pad for winter camping.

Bags, liners and pads are discussed in detail in Chapter 6.

Cold Weather Clothing

Remember that layering your clothing is of utmost importance when backpacking during the winter. Beginning with a layer of long underwear, you may want to add a warm shirt and pants, or a pile or fleece shirt and pants set. You can top these off with a layer that includes a warm parka and waterproof, insulated pants if it is really cold or a rain/wind suit if the temperature is only reasonably cold. Don't forget that you can add greatly to your warmth by donning a hat or balaclava.

If you are sufficiently bundled, the exertion of hiking should keep you warm. If you start feeling hypothermic, stop immediately, change into dry clothes if yours are wet, crawl into your sleeping bag and drink some hot liquid. Make sure the stove you bring will light (as well as boil water) in frigid weather.

Hypothermia is discussed in detail in Chapter 10. Remember that when hiking on open snow, it is wise to wear sunglasses because the sun reflecting off the bright, white snow can burn your eyes. Snowblindness can occur even on overcast days. If you don't have sunglasses, cut eye-slits in anything (a bandanna, for example) that can tie around your head. Should someone become snowblind, cold compresses, a painkiller and a lightproof bandage are needed. Between 18-20 hours later, the blindness should fade.

Water
Here are a few important tips that relate to water when hiking in snow or cold weather:

1) Never drink icy water in the winter or even on cool days. The cold water can cause your body temperature to drop. To avoid this, warm snow or water in your mouth before swallowing.

2) Protect your water when temperatures drop below freezing by burying it deep in your pack. At night, stash it inside your tent or at the end of your sleeping bag. You can also turn your water bottles upside down so that ice won't block the spout.

3) When hiking in deep snow, you can keep your bottles full of water by topping off with snow after each drink.

4) Use water to melt snow. An inch of water in your cook pot will melt snow more quickly. Add the crustiest, iciest or wettest snow to your pot—it will produce more water.

5) Keep in mind that melting snow will take more fuel and more time. With a cold wind blowing, it can take an hour and a stove full of fuel to melt and boil a quart of water.

6) It probably goes without saying to avoid yellow snow, but also steer clear of pink or "watermelon" snow. This snow

gets its name from its color, taste and scent produced by microrganisms that can cause diarrhea.

All the equipment needed for winter camping—warm clothes, four-season tents, sleeping bags, tent pegs, snow-shoes or skis–is available through outdoors stores where you will also find information on how to use the equipment.

A good reference book for camping in extremes such as snow and heat is *Harsh Weather Camping in the '90s* by Sam Curtis, published by Menasha Ridge Press.

When hiking in snow, rotate the trail-breaking duty among the hikers. It is easy to let yourself get tired and possibly careless if you push too hard.

◆ 13 ◆
Backpacking with Children

When we decided to take a backpacking trip along the A.T. to Grayson Highlands in Virginia, we told our daughter, Griffin, that she would probably see a number of wild ponies. She was thrilled. All the way from Georgia to Virginia, she repeated over and over, "Mama see wild horse, Papa see wild horse, Griffin see wild horse." And we would respond, "Yes, honey, we're all going to see the wild ponies."

When we finally settled Griffin in her backpack, I began to experience some trepidation. What if we didn't see any wild ponies? Griffin was so excited that I felt like a horse myself, as she urged me on, heels pressing into my ribs.

I had nothing to fear. We had hiked less than one hundred yards when we spied our first pony. From that point on, we nearly swam through ponies. When we set up camp, we soon had ponies surrounding our tent, nosing our backpacks, testing the strength of tent poles with their teeth. One pony, much to Griffin's delight, stuck her head in our tent.

Later, Griffin and I frolicked along with two young foals, racing along the grassy meadows of the Highlands. That night, as a sliver of a moon rose in the west, Griffin drifted off to sleep to the sound of thundering hooves, whickers and neighs.

For parents, the question often arises: Should you take your children hiking and backpacking on the A.T.?

Why not? Most children love the outdoors. I have vivid memories of camping with my family in the mountains of California that have led me to continue my love affair with nature.

I discovered my daughter's love for the outdoors when she was three months old. While attending a conference in San Diego, I found that Griffin fell asleep more quickly when I carried her around outside than she did when I walked her in our room. Maybe it was all those long walks I took trying to induce labor when she was two weeks overdue, but she blossoms when the wind caresses her face and the sun shines on her head. She even loves the sprinkle of rain and overcast skies! Since the conference and a subsequent tour of Muir Woods, she has graduated to a backpack and absolutely loves her new vantage point. We have dayhiked and backpacked along the A.T. many times since our trip to California.

From carrying a child in a pack, one can advance to having the child carry a pack, increasing the pack size and weight carried as the child grows.

Infants

The younger the child is, the more difficult the packing (except for ages four to six months when they have not yet learned to crawl). Younger than four months they don't yet fit in a pack, and after six, they take off as soon as they touch the ground. If possible, set up your tent before you put your child down; you will have a handy playpen to hold the child until you've set up camp.

Until the child is toilet-trained, you must carry diapers—disposable or otherwise. You'll have to pack them in and out. Cindy Ross suggests cloth diapers which she and her husband, Todd, dry on the back of their packs so that they are lighter to carry. When the child has a bowel movement, you can simply bury her poop as you would your own, fold up the diaper and carry it in a sealable plastic bag.

Because one person is carrying the child, the amount of extra stuff that person can carry is limited. This means the length of your trip is shortened though there are ways to get around that.

One option is to use the cache system and bury or hide extra diapers, food, etc. along the trail you plan to hike. Another option is to plan a hike where you know you'll be able to stop at stores often enough to pick up the items you'll need—more food and diapers. Yet another option is to send extra items to Post Offices along the way if you have steady access to them. Finally, there is the option of a support crew that meets you at road crossings with the extra things you need.

As for food, once the child has started on solids, it will make your trip a bit more difficult until she can eat what you eat without mashing, smashing, etc. If you plan meals that your child can eat, too, then you can bring along a hand grinder. Also, some health food stores offer dehydrated baby foods. Jars of baby food are a heavier option and will keep only a few days (less if it really hot outside) once the jar is opened.

If your child is still breastfeeding but not yet on solids, you're in a perfect situation for backpacking because you don't have to carry formula and bottles. Although difficult, formula-feeding is not impossible. Bottles can be heated on your cook stove the same way they would be heated on your stove at home—by warming them in water in your cook pot.

As for clothes, you know your child. Griffin tends to stay

on the warm side so we don't have to carry a lot of warm clothes for her when backpacking. Other babies stay cool and consequently the parents must bring extra layers of clothing for their child's comfort. Children can be layered as easily as adults. There are a lot of layering options for children. Many catalogs even offer miniature rain suits.

Since my child was due in the winter, I was anxious to find some warm clothes in a newborn size. I'll admit there wasn't much available, but I was able to find some red, cotton long johns. Less than 24 hours after Griffin's home birth, I dressed her in those very long johns for her first trip to the doctor. It was 20 degrees outside; the long johns were layered with a blanket sleeper and finally a fleece baby bag.

Keep in mind that there are many things infants under six months of age cannot do—such as wear sunscreen or insect repellent. If you are hiking in the sun, they need a wide-brimmed hat or a screen on their backpack. If your infant will wear them, there are sunglasses available in infant sizes. While still an infant, Griffin successfully wore the Flap-happy Hat sold by Biobottoms of California. The baseball-style cap had a wide front brim and a protective "flap" of material that covered her delicate neck. Patagonia makes a similar hat for infants and children.

When it comes time to bed down for the night, where do you put your infant? When Griffin was younger, I shared my bag with her but she is now too big for that. I have yet to find an infant-sized sleeping bag although some companies make bags designed to keep an infant warm that work well as sleeping bags. You may also want to try designing your own with a child-size down comforter or several blankets.

Some children, like Griffin, have no trouble falling asleep in a dark tent while others who wake to total darkness will freak-out. I always keep a flashlight handy should I need to comfort Griffin with a little light. Others may find the confining walls of a tent disconcerting and fuss, but usually they get used to a tent after a night or two.

Griffin Logue looks out of the tent on a backpacking trip to Grayson Highlands on the A.T. in Virginia.

Photo by Frank Logue

Keep in mind that a two-person tent is too small for the three of you, while a three-person tent will suit you for a long time.

I am only mentioning one child at this point; unless your second, third, etc. child(ren) can carry their own pack or hike entirely on their own, your backpacking will be limited to day hikes. Though llama packing is an option in some areas.

Toddlers

While you have basically the same concerns while backpacking with a toddler as you do with an infant, there is one major difference—they can walk.

Unfortunately, hiking for a toddler means two entirely different methods of movement: 1) Running, which usually ends up with the child on her face, especially on unlevel trails; and 2) Walking a few steps and then stopping to explore, walking a few steps then stopping to explore, walking a few . . . .

Both of these styles can result in frustration for the parent but are absolutely necessary for the sanity of your child. As much as Griffin loves her pack, she still needs to get out of it every once in awhile to stretch her new walking legs.

This means that they'll be eager to escape from their pack and hit the ground running. Once toddlers are out of the pack, though, they demand at least one set of eyes on them constantly. The outdoors is great for growing minds, but also poses certain dangers, especially if the child is still teething; everything she picks up is likely to end up in her mouth. She needs you to keep her from eating poison ivy, snails, deer droppings, etc.

Most packs for child carrying will hold your toddler until he reaches 35 to 40 pounds. After that, you will begin backpacking with . . .

Children

This will be a difficult stage, no doubt about it. Your child–even packless—will walk a hundred yards (if you're lucky) and then start complaining, weeping and wailing that he is tired. Remember that this is the same kid who can easily run the length of three football fields while playing with his friends.

When your child is at this stage, it is best to take frequent breaks until you reach your destination. You are thus limited to the number of miles you pack each day. No problem—just tone down your trips for awhile.

Your child can start with a fanny or daypack and carry his own toys and clothing. As your child gets older and stronger, you can move on to bigger packs and add food and sleeping bag to the gear he is carrying.

Gear

Outdoor Gear Manufacturers have discovered children in the 1990s. The amount of kid gear on the market has been steadily increasing during the decade.

Sleeping bags can be purchased for children between the sizes of 48 and 54 inches. From $40 to $100, a 15-degree or higher bag in the backpacker's mummy design is available. Griffin loves her Tough Traveler Growing Bear. It's a 25-degree bag that weighs 2 pounds and costs about $145. It grows from 39 to 55 inches with zip-on extensions. Other manufacturers making kid bags include Feathered Friends, Eastern Mountain Sports, Peak 1, REI and The North Face.

There are also packs designed especially for children as well as for parents who carry their children. Tough Traveler, Gerry and Kelty all make superb packs to carry your infant or toddler. Designed to hold kids up to 35 or 40 pounds, all include a pocket to carry diapers and other essentials for your baby. An optional rain/sunscreen can be purchased with the Tough Traveler as can extra pockets. Child carriers cost from $50 to $120.

Children's packs are made by a number of manufacturers, including Tough Traveler, REI, Kelty, Jansport, and Osprey. The Osprey Pika costs $95 and Tough Traveler's Camper costs about $105.

Manufacturers offer children's hiking boots, too! Vasque, Hi-Tec, Tecnica and others make hiking boots for children starting at about children's size ten. You can even find little boots for toddlers, but make sure they can actually walk in them before you purchase them for your child—they may be absolutely adorable but too rigid for a toddler's intrepid step. Hiking boots for children cost $30 to $50. When Griffin spent more time riding than walking, we had success with tough tennis shoes and non-name brand boots from discount shoe stores. That kept the cost down to about $15 to $20. Now her hiking style demands boots as rugged as our own.

Motivating Children

How can you make backpacking fun for your children and avoid the "how much farther" syndrome? The following are a few suggestions:

1) Revel in nature. Stop to point out interesting flowers, clouds, trees, mushrooms, etc. Enjoy water by throwing pebbles, floating sticks and leaves. Play in sand or mud or snow. Watch frogs hop, squirrels and chipmunks scuttle from tree to tree, insects crawling about, a deer standing stock still, a hawk drifting on air currents . . .
2) Teach your children geologic and natural history—that Indians once hunted in these woods, that they are walking on what was once hot lava, the intricacies of the glacier that molded this valley . . .
3) Answer your child's questions—Why is the sky blue? Are there still Indians in these woods? Will the volcano erupt on us? . . .
4) Get out the toys and a treat. Give your child a break with some fruit leather or a muffin and his or her favorite toy.

5) Promise a celebration when they have attained a certain goal—some juice and a piece of candy or if health-conscious, a fruit-sweetened cookie when you reach the top of the mountain or the next stream.

6) Play games that keep you moving. On slight inclines play Runaway Train by running wildly to the bottom of the hill (only if your child is capable of doing this without falling on his face); continue the train theme by pretending your family is a train, making the appropriate noises while walking. Try some other vehicle—airplane, ship, racecar, truck.

7) Tell stories. The parents can tell stories of past but true events, make up stories or even invite the children to tell a story. Asking questions of a child can also prolong their stamina.

8) Sing songs. Let the child choose or take turns choosing.

9) Play animals. Pick an animal and tell about it, makes its noises, etc.

10) Give them gorp. A handful of gorp for every 5, 10, 15, 20 steps (or whatever they're capable of) will keep them going for awhile.

At some point or another your child will pull the "I can't take another step without collapsing" trick. When the parent falls for this ploy and the child is carried to your destination, they usually experience a miracle upon arrival. The child's eyes spring open and she's off and running while the poor, exhausted parents later have to beg her to crawl into her sleeping bag.

On the other hand, children do not recognize fatigue and will drop from exhaustion before they show any true signs of tiring. Children are tough but not super-human. Don't push them too hard. Chances are, if you're tired, so are they.

If you want to get your children motivated before they hike, you might want to get a copy of the *Appalachian Trail Fun Book*. The coloring and activity book introduces four- to nine-year-olds to the A.T. It's published by the Appalachian Trail Conference, and available through them, as well as in bookstores and backpacking shops.

Limitations

Unless one partner is capable of carrying most of the gear (or in the case of a walking child, the parents can split most of the gear) you will have to put off any major backpacking trips until your child is old enough to take care of himself.

A single parent will have to limit his or her backpacking trips to dayhikes unless they intend to camp extra light (which is not really wise if you're hiking with children) by not carrying a tent, cookstove, etc.

You should be aware of your own limitations. If you can't regularly carry a 60-pound pack, don't think that you can do it if you have a child. If you normally carry a 40-pound pack and your child weighs 20 pounds, carry no more than 20 pounds of gear, for a total weight of 40 pounds of child and equipment. Remember, you have a life on your back now. Don't endanger it.

Introducing your child to the outdoors early does not necessarily mean they'll become avid backpackers later on, so don't be disappointed if they eventually lose interest.

If you want your children to grow to love hiking and the outdoors as you do, don't push too hard. If you try to do too much, they will only have unpleasant memories to fall back on. Be content just to get out on the trail, instead of setting big mileage goals.

◆ 14 ◆
Thru-Hiking

I go forth to make new demands on life. I wish to begin this summer well; to do something in it worthy of it and me; to transcend my daily routine and that of my townsmen . . . I pray that the life of this spring and summer may ever lie fair in my memory. May I dare as I have never done! May I persevere as I have never done!

-Henry David Thoreau

Thoreau's words echo the sentiments of many of the more than 1,000 people who set out each year intending to follow the white blazes from Georgia to Maine.

The ATC's definition of a thru-hiker is anyone who hikes the entire current Appalachian Trail in a single 12-month period. If you are thinking about hiking the entire Appalachian Trail, you may want to consider a few things first. Only 100 to 150 of those people make it the whole way in a single year; the other 90 percent must leave their dreams by the wayside. This happens for a number of reasons, but mostly because the trail turns out to be more than they bargained for.

Just about any person has the physical ability to hike the entire trail. It has been done by the young, the old, the handicapped and everybody in between. But physical ability is not all it takes. It is easy to romanticize hiking the Appalachian Trail as an easy walk in the woods. It is almost never easy, and it is never just a walk in the woods.

What It Takes to Be a Thru-hiker

"I started with the intention of finishing," explained Doug Davis. "I think a lot of the quitters only committed themselves to giving it a try. As I went along I would try to imagine finishing (my thru-hike). It was hard. I also tried to imagine not finishing. It was impossible."

Davis sums up the way most thru-hikers feel. It takes determination and goal orientation to finish the trail. Flexibility is the key.

Phil Hall said, "It takes determination, flexibility, and endurance. Without all three, you probably won't make it that far."

Before you begin planning your hike, ask yourself these questions.

- Will completing the trail be worth being wet/cold/hot day after day?
- Can I wear the same dirty clothes for days on end?
- Can I go without a bath, sometimes for as long as a week?
- Can I withstand the physical pain that often accompanies backpacking?
- Can I stand being away from my home/relationship for four to six months?
- Is the idea of thru-hiking the A.T. my all-consuming desire? Am I willing for it to be?
- Am I afraid of the outdoors—insects, animals, sleeping outdoors night after night?

Some of these questions may seem trivial, but all of them point to reasons that people quit the trail. Obviously, severe physical injuries and emergencies at home also are a factor, but these have nothing to do with the determination, flexibility and endurance it takes to hike the entire trail.

"Finishing the trail was all-important," said Sondra Davis, who hiked the trail with her husband, Craig. "But enjoying the trail was reason enough."

What do we mean by flexibility, endurance and determination? Consider this journal entry by Mac Wrightington penned at Vandeventer Shelter in Tennessee.

> First, the good news. Easy Ed (Ed Carlson) and I had a great time yesterday at Laurel Fork Shelter, and I slept fairly well despite reading in the register that a rat the size of a small dog resided there. I also had beautiful weather today.
>
> Now the bad (news). The guidebook's description of the store at 321 (limited supplies) was the understatement of the century. For the next two days, it's corn flakes and water for breakfast, cookies for lunch, and pork and beans for dinner. Also, my feet, that gave me trouble yesterday, are now dead. No, wait a minute, if they were dead they wouldn't hurt this bad. My trusty Raichles have finally given out on me—causing bruises, blisters, and bleeding. Damascus is 32 miles away now, should be an interesting couple of days ahead.

Wrightington didn't enjoy his problems, but he also didn't think about quitting. Every hiker has at least one day like Wrightington's, usually many more. It's just something you have to keep in mind when you intend to hike for four to six months. Like four to six months in the "real" world, something is bound to go wrong occasionally.

Why People Thru-hike

There is no one reason that draws people to hike the entire Appalachian Trail. But there does seem to be a common denominator among thru-hikers: they are mostly at some period of change in their lives. A divorce, graduation from college or high school, retirement, marriage, and an anticipated change of careers are all typical times that hikers take to the A.T. to follow it from end to end.

"One might conclude," said Bill Foot, "that the trail is a great place to figure out where to go or what to do with the rest of your life."

When and Where to Start

The majority of thru-hikers—about 90 percent—choose to start on Springer Mountain in Georgia and hike toward Mt. Katahdin in Maine. The rest start on Katahdin and head south. The reasons for starting in the South are fourfold: weather, blackflies, the One Hundred Mile Wilderness and loneliness. These are all problems to be contended with if you begin your hike on Mt. Katahdin, which will be lessened if you begin your hike on Springer Mountain.

Hiking South

The weather in Maine prohibits starting your trek before mid-May, at the earliest; snow can cover the Northern Appalachians well into spring. As the snow melts and the weather turns mild, the black flies descend on the Maine woods in droves. They are hard to see, all too easy to feel, and a real impediment to hiking before mid-July.

The One Hundred Mile Wilderness is the stretch of trail between Maine's Baxter State Park, the A.T.'s northern terminus, and Monson, Maine, which lies over 100 rugged miles to the south. For the out-of-shape hiker, Maine is a tough introduction to the trail. Carrying enough food to traverse the wilderness to Monson means hefting a heavier pack than will later be necessary.

Walking the full length of the Appalachian Trail will expose you to more of the trail's diversity than most hikers take advantage of. Here the white blazes guide a hiker through a residential neighborhood in Damascus, Virginia.

Photo by Frank Logue

Finally, there are fewer hikers heading south and your trip could be a solitary one. For some hikers this is the plus that makes up for a southbound hike's other difficulties; for others the loneliness can become a reason to leave the trail.

Hiking North

For potential thru-hikers leaving from Georgia, the date you begin your hike will determine the character of your trip. The Southern Appalachians can deal out heavy winter snows as late as mid-April. These storms usually are isolated and pass quickly, but cold weather can be pretty much counted on.

If you begin your thru-hike around the first week in March, you will have the trail largely to yourself. There will be more cold weather to deal with, but 60- to 70-degree days are not that uncommon either.

Between the middle of March and the middle of April you will meet up with more and more hikers. The largest group of potential thru-hikers starts around the first and second weeks in April. For the hiker in search of solitude, it may be worth braving the cold to leave in March. On the other hand, meeting hikers going through the same hardships can be encouraging, as Kurt Nielson explained.

"When it rains, it rains on all of us. We've all got the same rashes on our hips where our packs rub. Everybody's feet hurt. Everybody's shoulders hurt."

The Appalachian Trail is a social experience, and long-lasting friendships are often forged during a trip. If you're not interested in this aspect of trail life, you may want to hike another trail, hike south, or hike out of season—October through February—because even after the year's group of potential thru-hikers has passed, you will find yourself running into other hikers who are out for an overnight hike, a week, and more.

A lot of hikers who set out thinking of a thru-hike as a long, lone expedition find they enjoyed the camaraderie more than they anticipated. Dorothy Hansen, who runs the Walasi-yi center at Neel's Gap in Georgia with her husband, Jeff, said she intended for her hike to be a solitary experience. But setting out in early April she ended up hiking with a number of people, and upon finishing wouldn't have had it any other way.

Flip-flopping

Some thru-hikers find that they are not going to be able to make it to Katahdin before it closes for the winter (about October 15). There is another option rather than calling off your thru-hike—flip-flopping. In this case the thru-hiker leaves his or her north-bound hike in Harpers Ferry, West Virginia, for example, and travels north to Katahdin in Maine. Here, he or she begins a south-bound hike back to Harpers Ferry, thus completing the trail in one year.

Some hikers set out to flip-flop the trail because they feel it gives them more time, or because they cannot begin their hike until mid-summer and do not wish to hike entirely south-bound. Beginning mid-summer around Harpers Ferry allows them to hike with a good many of that year's north-bounders. Harpers Ferry is often a beginning or ending place because it is near the halfway point on the A.T.; it is also the location of the ATC headquarters.

Blue-blazing

Before you begin your thru-hike, you should make an important decision. Just what is the goal you are pursuing? Is it to hike the entire Appalachian Trail, or is it merely to spend several months hiking in the Appalachians? You should ask yourself this question because opportunities will arise to cut off sections of the trail to make it shorter, easier, or to provide easier access to shelters and towns.

The term for taking these shortcuts is blue-blazing. The name comes from the fact that most of the trails you will intersect are marked with blue blazes instead of the A.T.'s familiar white blazes. Hikers who stick to the white-blazed trail think of themselves as purists because they are staying true to their goal of hiking the entire trail.

If you decide ahead of time how "pure" you want your hike to be, you will have less trouble later. We discovered that once you begin to blue-blaze it is harder not to do so again.

The ATC does not take an official stand on blue-blazing. Most hikers consider it acceptable to take a loop trail to a shelter and come back to the white-blazed trail by the other side of the loop. This only cuts off .1 or .2 mile, and is common practice.

An example of an extreme case of blue-blazing would be

taking the Tuckerman Ravine trail down from Mt. Washington in New Hampshire to cut off the 12.9-mile hike across the Northern Presidential Range in less than 5 miles of downhill trail. So you can see that making a distinction before you leave home will help you chose which trail to follow once you're hiking. If you report to the Appalachian Trail Conference after your hike that you completed the trail, they will expect you to have hiked the entire current footpath. Obviously, it is on your conscience whether you have done so or not.

Whatever choice you make for yourself, remember that you are hiking for your own reasons and to meet your own goals. Allow others the same courtesy. Don't view another's hiking style for as wrong; it is only different.

2,000-milers

An alternative to thru-hiking the Appalachian Trail is to become a 2,000-miler. This is defined as anyone who completes the entire Appalachian Trail over a period of two or perhaps many more years.

If you are unable to take four to six months off for one long hike, you can break the trail up into smaller sections to be hiked over several years. The ATC doesn't make a distinction between 2,000-milers and thru-hikers, and the completion of the trail over many years is just as meaningful, if not more, than hiking the trail in one long hike.

How Much Does it Cost to Hike?

How much do you want it to cost? A good rough estimate is $1 a mile, not including any equipment you may need. This is not going cheap, nor is it extravagant. If you are careful, the Appalachian Trail can be a very inexpensive four to six months. Your only real cost is food, and some hikers include the equipment they must purchase in the $1 a mile estimate.

You don't have to stay in hostels. You can conceivably

camp instead of paying the few shelter fees. Other expenses include fuel for your stove. From there, what you spend is optional. Most hikers will splurge on restaurant meals when they go into town for food.

Other expenses might include:
- laundry and detergent
- entertainment (more batteries for your walkman, movies, dancing, books, magazines, etc.)
- an occasional hotel/motel stay
- replacement of gear (if you haven't already set aside a fund for emergencies)
- doctor bills (also an emergency fund item)
- miscellaneous items—batteries for your flashlight, stamps, stationery, etc.

Alcohol

There is something that is missing from the above list, and it's something that hikers tend to spend a lot of money on-alcohol. We don't intend to preach because, personally, there is nothing better to us than an ice-cold beer on a hot summer's day. Unfortunately, during the past decade the drinking of alcoholic beverages has gotten out of hand a number of times. The result is that hikers are no longer allowed in certain places. For example, some thru-hikers (in 1985) trashed and burned the floor of a community center in Dalton, Massachusetts. Fortunately, most thru-hikers are very well thought of; but it is always the few who ruin things for all. This isn't the most recent occurrence; several places have been closed to hikers in recent years.

Cash, Credit Cards or Traveler's Checks?

Hiking with up to $1,000 in cash is a bad way to test your trust in your fellow humans. Most hikers choose the safety and convenience of carrying traveler's checks. Traveler's checks can be cashed almost anywhere. We haven't heard of any store along the A.T., no matter how small or out-of-the-way, that wouldn't cash a traveler's check. By buying the checks in low denominations ($20) as well as larger checks of $100, you can assure that you won't be caught carrying a large amount of cash at any one time. For added peace of mind, and to help stay on-budget, it is a good idea to split your traveler's checks up into two or three groups to send to some of your mail drops.

Automated Teller Machines have made their way to many of the towns along the trail and have become a reliable way to receive money as well. Through credit cards or bank cards that are part of a nationwide network, such as Cirrus, hikers can obtain money in an emergency or as part of a scheduled withdrawal.

Whether you intend to use your credit card for cash withdrawals or not, plan to bring it along. A major credit card can be a lifesaver if equipment breaks or medical problems arise. Telephone company credit cards are helpful in reaching family and friends from the trail and can be used to contact equipment manufacturers in an emergency.

Insurance

Setting out to hike the length of the Appalachian Trail without medical insurance is folly at best, though many hikers, ourselves included, take this route. Comparably low-cost, short-term medical insurance is available through most companies. The short-term policies are designed for people between jobs and typically last no longer than six months. This type of policy is nonrenewable but allows enough coverage for the duration of an A.T. thru-hike. As with any policy, the higher the deductible, the lower the premiums will be.

Mail Drops

Even if you don't intend to send your food ahead, you should plan a few mail drops. Sending film, guidebooks and maps,

Sno-Seal, seam sealer, or other hard-to-buy items is just one use for a mail drop. Friends and family can be given a list of post offices where you will plan to check for mail. This usually produces a variety of letters and packages, making all your planning worthwhile.

Packages should be addressed to you, General Delivery, and list the city, state, and zip code of the post office. By having the letters and packages marked "Hold for North-bound (or South-bound) A.T. Thru-hiker," you will ensure that the post office will hold them much longer than customary. Post offices that are frequented by hikers generally hold mail until that year's group of hikers stops coming by, before returning to sender. Zip codes for post offices near the trail and distances from the trail to the post office are given in the annually updated *Data Book* published by the Appalachian Trail Conference. Another resource for planning your mail drops is *The Appalachian Trail Workbook for Planning Thru-hikes*, which is also published by A.T.C.

As nice as receiving mail can be, remember that mail drops can also be a nuisance. If you come in to a town after noon on Saturday, you will probably have to wait until Monday morning for mail. If the mail drop is not essential, you can send or leave a forwarding card and let the mail catch up to you later. Using a number of mail drops for food or any other essential (e.g., money) will mean that you will have to schedule your hike around getting to town when the post office is open.

Spacing your post office pick-ups about 150 to 200 miles apart should be sufficient if you don't use them as your only source of food.

Hiking Partners

Many people who wish to hike the entire length of the Applachian Trail do not wish to do so alone. Is it possible to find an appropriate partner? Possible, yes. Easy, no.

Most potential thru-hikers search for a partner by either

placing an ad in the *Appalachian Trailway News* (ads are free to members, but "personal" ads are refused) or by answering an ad in the same publication. According to Judy Jenner, editor of the ATN, people nearly always find a partner. But, she said, few remain with the partner they find in the ads.

"Everyone seemed to agree that the decision to place or answer an ad was a good one," she said. "On the other hand, most said the partnership didn't last the length of the hike."

But, if finding a partner through an ad will get you out on the trail it is definitely worth the effort. At least until you gain the confidence to either hike on your own or until you hook up with a new partner.

If you don't want to find a partner through an ad, you can easily find people to hike with by starting your thru-hike during peak hiking season—April 1 through mid-May. During this time there are so many potential thru-hikers starting out that whether you like it or not, you'll be sharing shelters and trail nearly all the way to Maine.

Some more advice:

"Undertaking a thru-hike with another person is a more intense experience than marriage," said Bill O'Brien, who hiked with Andrew Sam. "At least in marriage, you each presumably go off to work at different jobs. On a thru-hike, you're together always, day and night."

Andrew Sam agreed, adding, "Don't feel obligated to hike together during the day. Meet up at lunch and at a campsite. Above all, be flexible."

"It's sometimes very difficult to hike with someone else, mainly because of different paces," said Joe Cook who hiked with his wife, Monica. "And, being with the same person literally every minute of the day can become tiring. Don't be afraid to split up for part of the day."

Some couples don't mind the constant companionship. Cal and Mary Batchelder recommend, "If you wish to hike right behind each other (but not too close), hike at the slowest hiker's pace." Frank and I thru-hiked this way, successfully.

Mailing Gear Ahead

One way to use the mail system to your advantage is to send equipment further down the trail instead of home.

"One of the most helpful things I did for myself about a third of the way through the trip was to have a box that I continually sent ahead of myself," said Rob White. "I used the box to carry excess equipment up the trail for me. And when I decided to get rid of my tent and use the tarp, I sent the tent about a week ahead before I sent it home."

This technique can be used for extra food, contact lens solution, clothing, soap, resealable plastic bags and more. The postage cost can add up, but if you're thinking of doing without some piece of equipment, this is the best way to try going without it.

The Appalachian Trail Companion

The Appalachian Trail Companion, published annually by the Appalachian Trail Conference, offers a wealth of information to long-distance hikers on goods and services available along the trail and much more. The guide is edited by the Appalachian Long Distance Hikers Association. The information in the book is compiled from information supplied by thru-hikers and others at the end of every year for the following spring.

The Appalachian Trail Companion will help you to decipher the information in the *Data Book* by telling you more about the places, such as grocery stores, than the letter code in the *Data Book* conveys.

Hostels

A hostel can be as simple as the floor of a church or barn, or it may offer as much as a hot shower, warm bed, laundry facilities and food. Hostels range in price from free (although a donation is always appreciated) to $20 or more a night. All offer a deal to hikers that shouldn't be taken advantage of. It is a good idea to limit your stay to a night or two (unless it's

"The Place" in Damascus, Virginia is one of the best known of the hostels available to A.T. hikers. The United Methodist Church in Damascus has operated this house behind the church as a hostel since 1976.

Photo by Frank Logue

an emergency) if the hostel is run by volunteers on a donation basis.

If you intend to stay in hostels during a thru-hike, count on leaving at least a small donation (especially if they don't ask for it). One hostel received not a penny from 1989's north-bounders but received at least $1 and as much as $6 from each of the same year's south-bounders, a much smaller group. Some hostels will let you work off your stay, but all appreciate a helping hand even if you're paying. If the hostel is a business, you need only to be courteous and may stay as long as you are willing to pay for a room or bed; but if it is run by volunteers, help out. Prove that thru-hikers are not the socially irresponsible crowd a lot of people think we are. Try to clean up behind other hikers as well as yourself. A good attitude goes a long way toward improving relations along the Appalachian Trail.

A current listing of hostels can be found in *The Appalachian Trail Companion*.

Organizations

Appalachian Long Distance Hikers Association
ALDHA is the only organization of long distance hikers in the United States. Although its focus is on the Appalachian Trail, ALDHA also promotes long distance trails around the world. For those interested in hiking the A.T., ALDHA is a great organization to join. Each year, ALDHA hosts The Gathering of Long Distance Hikers. But, The Gathering is not limited to those who have hiked the Appalachian and other trails. Future hikers and hiker and trail helpers also attend.

For $17, hikers are treated to a Columbus Day weekend of workshops (including an extensive workshop on preparing for an A.T. hike), slideshows, music and dancing, and the camaraderie of hikers and hiker friends. A campsite is included in the fee, but meals are extra. The fee includes a $7 annual membership in ALDHA. ALDHA members receive a quarterly newsletter, *The Long Distnce Hiker*, and an membership directory.

The Appalachian Trail Conference
Hikers dreaming of hiking all or part of the Appalachian Trail are advised to join the Appalachian Trail Conference. A membership in the ATC ($25 for a single, $30 for a family) includes a subscription to *Appalachian Trailway News* and a discount on books, t-shirts and other items sold by the Conference. The ATC also hosts a biennial meeting in odd numbered years.

Membership in the Conference also gives you the satisfaction of supporting the organization responsible for the protection and maintenance of the Appalachian Trail.

While on the Trail

Bob Dowling suggests the following to keep your mind centered on a thru-hike:

1) Be sure of your reasons for doing the trail. Write them down somewhere, and check them occasionally to see if they are still valid.

2) Take breaks every so often in hostels, trail towns, or even on the trail. These days of rest and pampering yourself are very important both physically and mentally.

3) The trail is too long to set as a goal. Split it up into sections or states, and celebrate each goal accomplished.

Important Final Note on Planning a Thru-Hike

Proper planning is essential for any long distance hike on the Appalachian Trail, but don't take it too far. "There's such a thing as doing too much research," offers thru-hiker Joe Cook. "If you know what's around every curve in the trail, you have missed out on one of the most exciting parts of a thru-hike. Also rely on your own instincts and experience to guide you along the trail."

The Afterlife

Once you've hiked the entire trail, you will find that things will never be quite the same again. The trail's effect is different on each hiker, but no one is left unchanged.

For example: "I still am having trouble (adjusting to life off the trail)," said Kurt Nielsen, several months after he had finished. "It was such a life-changing episode and I miss the simple life and my trail buddies."

"Before I left (to hike the trail) I had everything ahead of me," said Peter Scal. "Now I'm trying to recapture the feeling by choosing a new goal."

Helen Gray stands on top of the sign on Katahdin's Baxter Peak, which marks the northern terminus of the Appalachian Trail. Gray had just completed a 2,100-mile thru-hike of the A.T.

Photo by Frank Logue

"Too many things hit you," said Todd Gladfelter, "bills, phone, cars, appointments."

These changes often lead to a change of life-style, and sometimes a change of career.

"I'm not going back to office work or pressure work," said Nancy Hill. "I'm going to have a cleaning business and clean houses—my own hours with flexibility."

Or, as Bob Dowling put it: "Hiking the Appalachian Trail made me realize the virtue in a simple life-style. Shelter and food are all that is really necessary."

◆ Appendix 1 ◆
Equipment Checklists

Equipment for a Day Hike
(This list assumes you are already wearing comfortable
clothes and good walking shoes)

Day pack or fanny pack
One-liter (minimum) canteen
Rain gear
Food for the day
Lighter or waterproof matches
First aid (bandages, moleskin)
Toilet paper, trowel
Map and/or guidebook*
Camera and film*
Binoculars*
Gloves and knit cap+
Extra shirt+
Bandana*

Equipment for an Overnight Hike
Light or medium weight hiking boots
Internal or external frame pack
Sleeping bag
Sleeping pad
Tent/tarp and groundcloth
Lighter and/or waterproof matches
Stove and fuel
Cooking pot and eating utensils
Knife (pocket)

Water purifiers (or plan to boil your water)
More than adequate food for length of hike
Spices*
One-liter (minimum) canteen
Drinking cup
Rain gear including pack cover
Gaiters*
One pair of shorts
One pair of loose fitting, long pants+
One to two short sleeve shirts
One long sleeve shirt or sweater
Knit cap
Two pairs liner socks
Two pairs socks
One or more bandanas
Long johns+
Parka (down or synthetic fill)+
Underwear (2 pair)*
Toilet paper, trowel
Biodegradable soap and washcloth
Deodorant*
Toothbrush and toothpaste
Shaving kit*
Nylon cord (at least 10 feet)
Maps, guidebooks, or *Data Book*
Compass*
Flashlight with new batteries
Watch or clock*
Sunglasses*
First Aid kit (including moleskin)
Space blanket
Swimsuit and towel*
Extra shoes*
Repair equipment (for pack, tent, and stove)*
Camera and film*

Radio with headphones*
Insect repellent+
Sunscreen/lotion+
Hiking stick*

Additional Equipment Needed for Longer Hikes
Repair equipment for pack, tent, stove, and clothes
Trash bag (a small one for your own trash)
Long sleeved shirt or sweater
Long johns
Film mailers*
*The Appalachian Trail Companion**
Reading material*
Journal*

*Optional
+Seasonal

◆ Appendix 2 ◆
Books About The Appalachian Trail

The following books are available from the Appalachian Trail Conference, P.O. Box 807, Harpers Ferry, WV 25425-0807 as well as outdoor retailers and bookstores.

2,000 Miles on the Appalachian Trail, by Don Fortunato.
An illustrated account of an early 1970s thru-hike.

The New Appalachian Trail: Appalachian Hiker III, by Ed Garvey.
Written by well-known Appalachian Trail guru, Ed Garvey, this book is an account of his 1990 attempt at a second thru-hike at the age of seventy-five. Includes timeless advice on thru-hiking.

The Appalachian National Scenic Trail: A Time to be Bold, by Dr. Charles H. W. Foster.
A history of the trail and its public protection.

The Appalachian Trail Thru-hikers' Companion, edited by the Appalachian Long Distance Hikers Association.
An annually updated companion to the Data Book for long distance hikers. The on-trail guide gives details on what services are available along the trail and more.

Appalachian Trail Data Book, compiled by Daniel D. Chazin.
An annually updated guide pinpointing mileages between features and facilities on the trail.

Appalachian Trail Fun Book, by Frank and Victoria Logue.
A 72-page coloring and activity book designed to introduce four- to nine-year-olds to the Appalachian Trail.

Appalachian Trail Guides, published by the Appalachian Trail Conference.

The eleven official trail guides are published by the ATC or its member clubs and are updated every two to three years, in most cases. Each guide is a pocket-sized book detailing a section of trail and comes with topographic maps of that section. All guides are sold in a waterproof plastic pouch.

Maine, Revised 1996
New Hampshire/Vermont, Revised 1998
Massachusetts/Connecticut, Revised 1996
New York/New Jersey, Revised 1998
Pennsylvania, Revised 1998
Maryland/Northern Virginia, Revised 1995
Shenandoah National Park, Revised 1994
Central Virginia, Revised 1994
Southwest Virginia, Revised 1998
Tennessee/North Carolina, Revised 1995
North Carolina/Georgia, Revised 1998

The Appalachian Trail: A Visitor's Companion, by Leonard Adkins.

This book presents an overview of the geology, history, flora, and fauna of the Appalachian Trail.

The Appalachian Trail Workbook for Planning Thru-hikes, by Chris Whalen.

A rip-out-the-pages workbook of checklists, maildrop, etc.

As Far as the Eye Can See, by David Brill.

A well-written and reflective account of a 1978 thru-hiker.

Backpacking in the 90s, by Frank and Victoria Logue.

Offers everything there is to know about backpacking. A goof companion piece to *The Appalachian Trail Backpacker*.

The Best of the Appalachian Trail: Day Hikes, by Frank and Victoria Logue.

This book describes over one hundred hikes along the Appalachian Trail you can hike in a day.

The Best of the Appalachian Trail: Overnight Hikes, by Frank and Victoria Logue.

This book describes 60 of the best hikes along the Appalachian Trail you can take over the course of a weekend.

Blind Courage: Journey of Faith, by Bill Irwin and David McCasland.

A stirring account of a blind hiker's 1990 thru-hike of the A.T. with his dog, Orient.

A Journey of Friendship: A Thru-hike on the Appalachian Trail, by Melody A. Blaney and L. K. Ullyart.

An account of a 1996 thru-hike by two women who "met" through the *Appalachian Trailway News*.

Katahdin with Love: An Inspirational Journey, by Madelaine Cornelius.

A couple's story of their A.T. thru-hike begun after the death of their son.

A Season on the Trail, by Lynn Setzer.

This book contains the thoughts and experiences of 1996 thru-hikers, gathered from trail registers, postcards, and personal interviews.

Underfoot: A Geologic Guide to the Appalachian Trail, by V. Collins Chew.

A guide to the geology of the entire Appalachian Trail, including a history of the formation of the Appalachian Mountain chain.

Walking with Spring, by Earl Shaffer.

Shaffer's story of his 1948 thru-hike. Shaffer was the first to hike the entire Appalachian Trail in a single year.

A Woman's Journey, by Cindy Ross.

The personal story of Ross's two-year, 2,100-mile journey on the A.T. in the late 1970s.

◆ Appendix 3 ◆
Suppliers of Backpacking Equipment

The following is by no means a complete list of manufacturers of backpacking equipment. But it should give those interested in purchasing equipment a place to start. Some of the more significant products that the manufacturers sell are listed in parenthesis. Not all equipment offered by these manufacturers is listed.

Asolo USA, 190 Hanover Street, Lebanon, NH 03766. Phone: (603) 448-8827. (Boots)

Bibler Tents/Black Diamond Equipment, Ltd., 2084 East 3900 South, Salt Lake City, UT 84124. Phone: (801) 278-5533. (Tents, sleeping bags, butane stove)

Camping Gaz/Suunto USA, 2151 Las Palmas Drive, Suite G, Carlsbad, CA 92009. Phone: (800) 543-9124. (Butane stoves, Katadyn filters, lanterns)

Campmor, P.O. Box 700, Upper Saddle River, NJ 07458. Phone: (800) 525-4784. (Distributor of a wide variety of hiking equipment, including Campmor brand products.)

Caribou Mountaineering, Inc., 400 Commerce Road, Alice, TX 78332. Phone: (800) 824-4153. (Packs, sleeping bags)

Dana Design, 19215 Vashon Highway S.W., Vashon, WA 98070. Phone: (888) 357-3262. (Packs)

Diamond Brand, P.O. Box 249, Naples, NC 28760. Phone: (800) 258-9811. (Packs, tents)

Eastern Mountain Sports, One Vose Farm Road, Peterborough, NH 03458. Phone: (888) 463-6367. (Distributor of a wide variety of hiking equipment, including EMS brand products.)

Eureka!/JWA, 625 Conklin Road, Binghamton, NY 13903. Phone: (800) 572-8822. (Tents, backpacks)

Feathered Friends, 409 Yale Aveneu North, Seattle, WA 98109. Phone: (206) 292-6292. (Down sleeping bags)

Foam Designs Consumer Products, Inc., P.O. Box 11184, Lexington, KY 40581. Phone: (606) 231-7006. (Sleeping pads)

General Ecology, 151 Sheree Boulevard, Exton, PA 19341. Phone: (800) 441-8166. (First Need brand water purifiers)

Gregory Mountain Products, 100 Calle Cortez, Temecula, CA 92590. Phone: (800) 477-3420; Customer Service Phone, (800) 854-8585. (Internal frame packs, tents)

Hi-Tec, 4801 Stoddard Road, Modesto, CA 95356. Phone: (800) 521-1698. (Lightweight boots)

Jansport, 10411 Airport Road, Everett, WA 98204. Phone: (800) 552-6776; Customer Service Phone, (800) 426-9227. (Packs)

Kelty, Inc., 6235 G Lookout Road, Boulder, CO 80301. Phone: (800) 423-2320. (Packs, child carrier, sleeping bags, tents)

Koflach/Atomic For Sport, 9 Columbia Drive, Amherst, NH 03031. Phone: (800) 258-5020. (Heavyweight boots)

Peter Limmer & Sons, Inc., Route 16A, Intervale, NH 03845. Phone: (603) 356-5378. (Stock and custom-made boots, boot repair)

L.L. Bean, Casco Street, Freeport, ME 04033-0001. Phone: (800) 809-7057; Customer Service Phone, (800) 341-4341. (Distributor of a wide variety of hiking equipment, including L.L. Bean brand products.)

Lowe Alpine Systems, 2325 W. Midway Boulevard, Broomfield, CO 80020. Phone: (303) 465-0522; Customer Service Phone, (303) 465-3706. (Packs)

Merrell Outdoor Footwear, 9341 Courtland Drive NE, Rockford, MI 49351. Phone: (888) 637-7001. (Boots)

Moonstone Mountain Equipment, 833 Indiana Street, San Francisco, CA 94107. Phone: (800) 390-3312. (Sleeping bags)

Moss Tents, P.O. Box 577, Camden, ME 04843. Phone: (800) 859-5322. (Tents)

Mountain Safety Research (MSR), P.O. Box 24547, Seattle, WA 98124. Phone: (800) 877-9677. (Stoves with both the MSR name and Trangia brand; water purifiers)

Mountainsmith, Inc., 18301 West Colfax Avenue, Heritage Square, Building P, Golden, CO 80401. Phone: (800) 426-4075. (Packs, tents)

Nike, Inc., 1 Bowerman Drive, Beaverton, OR 97005. Phone: (800) 238-6453; Customer Service Phone,: (800) 344-6453. (Lightweight boots, rain gear, outdoor wear)

The North Face, 2013 Farallon Drive, San Leandro, CA 94577. Phone: (800) 719-6678. (Packs, tents, sleeping bags, outdoor wear)

Montrail Footwear, 1003 Sixth Avenue South, Seattle, WA 98134. Phone: (206) 621-9303. (Boots)

Optimus/Suunto USA, 2151 Las Palmas Drive, Carlsbad, CA 92009. Phone: (800) 543-9124. (White gas and kerosene stoves)

Patagonia, 8550 White Fir Street, Reno, NV 89533-2050. Phone: (800) 638-6464. (Outdoor wear)

Peak 1/The Coleman Company, Inc., P.O. Box 2931, Wichita, KS 67201. Phone: (800) 835-3278. (Packs, sleeping bags, white gas and multifuel stoves)

PUR, 9300 75th Avenue North, Minneapolis, MN 55428. Phone: (800) 787-5463. (Water filters)

REI (Recreational Equipment, Inc.), 1700 45th Street E, Sumner, WA 98390-0800. Phone: (800) 426-4840; Customer service phone, (800) 828-5533. (Distributor of a wide variety of hiking equipment, including REI brand products.)

Sierra Designs, 1255 Powell Street, Emeryville, CA 94608. Phone: (800) 635-0461; Customer Service, (800) 736-8551. (Tents, rain gear, sleeping bags)

Therm-a-Rest by Cascade Designs, Inc., First Avenue South, Seattle, WA 98134. Phone: (800) 531-9531. (Sleeping bags and pads)

Vasque, 314 Main Street, Red Wing, MN 55066. Phone: (800) 224-4453; Customer Service Phone, (800) 842-1301. (Lightweight and medium-weight boots)

VauDe Sports, Inc., P.O. Box 3413, Mammoth Lakes, CA 93546. Phone: (800) 447-1539. (Packs, sleeping bags, tents, outdoor wear)

ZZ Manufacturing, Inc., 1520 A Industrial Park Street, Corina, CA 91722. Phone: (800) 594-9046. (Battery-powered, wood-burning backpacking stoves)

◆ Appendix 4 ◆
Trail Maintenance Clubs

The Appalachian Trail owes its existence to the hiking clubs, which are charged with its maintenance. These clubs are responsible not only for the maintenance of the footpath but also for relocating the trail, managing its surrounding lands, helping with land acquisition negotiations, compiling and updating guidebook and map information, working with trail communities on both problems and special events, and recruiting and training new maintainers.

The clubs also sponsor backpacking and hiking trips as well as workshops. These are a great way to meet others interested in hiking.

The following list contains the names and trail assignments of clubs along the Appalachian Trail. Addresses appear for those with permanent offices or post office boxes. In other cases, please contact ATC headquarters for the address of the current club president or other appropriate officer (P.O. Box 807, Harpers Ferry, West Virginia, 25425).

Maine Appalachian Trail Club, P.O. Box 283, Augusta, ME 04330.

MATC covers 268.8 miles from Katahdin to ME 26 (Grafton Notch, ME).

Appalachian Mountain Club, 5 Joy Street, Boston, MA 02108.

AMC covers 118.8 miles from Grafton Notch, ME. to Kinsman Notch, NH.

Dartmouth Outing Club, P.O. Box 9, Hanover, NH 03755.

DOC covers 76.3 miles from Kinsman Notch, NH. to VT 12.

Green Mountain Club, Rural Route 1, Box 650, Waterbury Center, VT 05677.

GMC covers 121.8 miles from VT 12 to the Massachusetts border.

AMC—Berkshire Chapter, P.O. Box 2088, Pittsfield, MA 02201.

The Berkshire Chapter covers 86.5 miles from the Vermont border to Sages Ravine, MA.

AMC—Connecticut Chapter, 472 Burlington Avenue, Bristol, CT 06010.

The Connecticut Chapter covers 47.5 miles from Sages Ravine, MA, to the New York border.

The New York–New Jersey Trail Conference, 232 Madison Avenue, Room 802, New York, NY 10016.

NY–NJTC covers 166.9 miles from the Connecticut border to Delaware Water Gap, PA.

Keystone Trails Association, P.O. Box 251, Cogan Station, PA 17728.

KTA is the blanket association for the following 10 independent trail clubs, all of which can be contacted at the above address.

Wilmington Trail Club: 7.2 miles from Delaware Water Gap, PA, to Fox Gap, PA.

Batona Hiking Club: 11.2 miles from Fox Gap, PA, to Wind Gap, PA.

AMC—Delaware Valley Chapter: 15.5 miles from Wind Gap, PA, to Little Gap, PA.

Philadelphia Trail Club: 10.2 miles from Little Gap, PA, to Lehigh Furnace Gap, PA.

Blue Mountain Eagle Climbing Club: Split into two sections—64.4 miles from Lehigh Furnace Gap, PA, to Bake Oven Knob, PA, and from Tri-County Corner, PA, to Rausch Creek, PA.

Allentown Hiking Club: 11.7 miles from Bake Oven Knob, PA, to Tri-County Corner, PA.

Brandywine Valley Outing Club: 11.2 miles from Rausch Creek, PA, to PA 325.

Susquehanna Appalachian Trail Club: 9.2 miles from PA 325 to PA 225.

York Hiking Club: 7.8 miles from PA 225 to the Susquehanna River.

Cumberland Valley Appalachian Trail Management Association: 18 miles from Darlington Trail to Center Point Knob.

Mountain Club of Maryland, 1030 Goff Road, Baltimore, MD 21221.
The MCM covers 28.5 miles from the Susquehanna River to Darlington Trail and from Center Point Knob to Pine Grove Furnace State Park, PA.

Potomac Appalachian Trail Club, 118 Park Street S.E., Vienna, VA 22180-4609.
The PATC covers 240 miles from Pine Grove Furnace State Park, PA, to Rockfish Gap, VA.

Old Dominion Appalachian Trail Club, P.O. Box 25283, Richmond, VA 23260-5283.

ODATC covers 17 miles from Rockfish Gap, VA, to Reeds Gap, VA.

Tidewater Appalachian Trail Club, P.O. Box 8246, Norfolk, VA 23503.

Tidewater covers 10.5 miles from Reeds Gap, VA, to Tye River, VA.

Natural Bridge Appalachian Trail Club, P.O. Box 3012, Lynchburg, VA 24503.

NBATC covers 87.9 miles from the Tye River, VA, to Black Horse Gap, VA.

Roanoke Appalachian Trail Club, P.O. Box 12282, Roanoke, VA 24024.

RATC covers 131.2 miles from Black Horse Gap, VA, to VA 608.

Virginia Tech Outing Club, P.O. Box 538, Blacksburg, VA 24060.

Virginia Tech covers 29.6 miles from VA 608 to Garden Mountain, VA.

Piedmont Appalachian Trail Hikers, P.O. Box 4423, Greensboro, NC 27404.

PATH covers 57 miles from Garden Mountain, VA, to VA 670.

Mount Rogers Appalachian Trail Club, 24198 Greenspring Road, Abingdon, VA 28802.

Mount Rogers covers 56.2 miles from VA 670 to Damascus, VA.

Tennessee Eastman Hiking Club, P.O. Box 511, Kingsport, TN 37662.

TEHC covers 125.3 miles from Damascus, VA, to Spivey Gap, NC.

Carolina Mountain Club, P.O. Box 68, Asheville, NC 28802.

CMC covers 90.1 miles from Spivey Gap, NC, to Davenport Gap, TN/NC.

The Smoky Mountains Hiking Club, P.O. Box 1454, Knoxville, TN 37901.

SMHC covers 97.4 miles from Davenport Gap, TN/NC, to the Nantahala River, NC.

Nantahala Hiking Club, 173 Carl Slagle Road, Franklin, NC 28734.

NHC covers 60 miles from the Nantahala River to Bly Gap on the Georgia border.

Georgia Appalachian Trail Club, P.O. Box 654, Atlanta, GA 30301.

GATC covers 77.5 miles from the North Carolina border to Springer Mountain.

Two other groups of note:
American Hiking Society, 1422 Fenwick Lane, Silver Spring, MD 20910

A nationwide group promoting hiking and trails in America. Among many other projects, they were instrumental in the creation of the coast-to-coast American Discovery Trail and of National Trail Day.

Appalachian Long Distance Hikers Association, 10 Benning Street, Box 224, West Lebanon, NH 03784.

ALDHA sponsors the annual Gathering of Long Distance Hikers as well as trail maintenance trips.

✦ Index ✦

◆ About the authors ◆

Victoria and Frank Logue hiked the entire Appalachian Trail in 1988. They have returned again and again to hike it in its many parts on day and overnight hikes. They are the authors of *The Appalachian Trail Backpacker's Planning Guide, The Best of The Appalachian Trail: Dayhikes, The Best of the Appalachian Trail: Overnight Hikes* and the *Appalachian Trail Fun Book.* Victoria Logue is also the author of *Backpacking in the '90s: Tips, Techniques and Secrets* and *Camping in the 90s: Tips, Techniques and Secrets.*

They live in northern Virginia, where they enjoy sharing their love of nature with their daughter, Griffin. The Logues can be found online at http://members.aol.com/franklogue

◆ *Colophon* ◆

The text in this book was set in a digital version of the classic typeface New Baskerville. The typeface was first cut in the 1750's by John Baskerville, a printer in Birmingham, England. The book was designed and composed by Carolina Graphics Group of Rome, Georgia.